Digital Business Model
Complete Self-Assessment Guide

The guidance in this Self-Assessment is based on Digital Business Model best practices and standards in business process architecture, design and quality management. The guidance is also based on the professional judgment of the individual collaborators listed in the Acknowledgments.

Table of Contents

About The Art of Service

The Art of Service, Business Process Architects since 2000, is dedicated to helping stakeholders achieve excellence.

Defining, designing, creating, and implementing a process to solve a stakeholders challenge or meet an objective is the most valuable role… In EVERY group, company, organization and department.

Unless you're talking a one-time, single-use project, there should be a process. Whether that process is managed and implemented by humans, AI, or a combination of the two, it needs to be designed by someone with a complex enough perspective to ask the right questions.

Someone capable of asking the right questions and step back and say, 'What are we really trying to accomplish here? And is there a different way to look at it?'

With The Art of Service's Standard Requirements Self-Assessments, we empower people who can do just that — whether their title is marketer, entrepreneur, manager, salesperson, consultant, Business Process Manager, executive assistant, IT Manager, CIO etc... —they are the people who rule the future. They are people who watch the process as it happens, and ask the right questions to make the process work better.

Contact us when you need any support with this Self-Assessment and any help with templates, blue-prints and examples of standard documents you might need:

http://theartofservice.com
service@theartofservice.com

Acknowledgments

This checklist was developed under the auspices of The Art of Service, chaired by Gerardus Blokdyk.

Representatives from several client companies participated in the preparation of this Self-Assessment.

In addition, we are thankful for the design and printing services provided.

Included Resources - how to access

Included with your purchase of the book is the Digital Business Model Self-Assessment Spreadsheet Dashboard which contains all questions and Self-Assessment areas and auto-generates insights, graphs, and project RACI planning - all with examples to get you started right away.

How? Simply send an email to
access@theartofservice.com
with this books' title in the subject to get the Digital Business Model Self Assessment Tool right away.

You will receive the following contents with New and Updated specific criteria:

- The latest quick edition of the book in PDF

- The latest complete edition of the book in PDF, which criteria correspond to the criteria in...

- The Self-Assessment Excel Dashboard, and...

- Example pre-filled Self-Assessment Excel Dashboard to get familiar with results generation

- In-depth specific Checklists covering the topic

- Project management checklists and templates to assist with implementation

INCLUDES LIFETIME SELF ASSESSMENT UPDATES

Every self assessment comes with Lifetime Updates and Lifetime Free Updated Books. Lifetime Updates is an industry-first feature which allows you to receive verified self assessment updates, ensuring you always have the most accurate information at your fingertips.

Get it now- you will be glad you did - do it now, before you forget.

Send an email to **access@theartofservice.com** with this books' title in the subject to get the Digital Business Model Self Assessment Tool right away.

Your feedback is invaluable to us

If you recently bought this book, we would love to hear from you! You can do this by writing a review on amazon (or the online store where you purchased this book) about your last purchase! As part of our continual service improvement process, we love to hear real client experiences and feedback.

How does it work?
To post a review on Amazon, just log in to your account and click on the Create Your Own Review button (under Customer Reviews) of the relevant product page. You can find examples of product reviews in Amazon. If you purchased from another online store, simply follow their procedures.

What happens when I submit my review?
Once you have submitted your review, send us an email at review@theartofservice.com with the link to your review so we can properly thank you for your feedback.

Purpose of this Self-Assessment

This Self-Assessment has been developed to improve understanding of the requirements and elements of Digital Business Model, based on best practices and standards in business process architecture, design and quality management.

It is designed to allow for a rapid Self-Assessment to determine how closely existing management practices and procedures correspond to the elements of the Self-Assessment.

The criteria of requirements and elements of Digital Business Model have been rephrased in the format of a Self-Assessment questionnaire, with a seven-criterion scoring system, as explained in this document.

In this format, even with limited background knowledge of Digital

Business Model, a manager can quickly review existing operations to determine how they measure up to the standards. This in turn can serve as the starting point of a 'gap analysis' to identify management tools or system elements that might usefully be implemented in the organization to help improve overall performance.

How to use the Self-Assessment

On the following pages are a series of questions to identify to what extent your Digital Business Model initiative is complete in comparison to the requirements set in standards.

To facilitate answering the questions, there is a space in front of each question to enter a score on a scale of '1' to '5'.

1 Strongly Disagree

2 Disagree

3 Neutral

4 Agree

5 Strongly Agree

Read the question and rate it with the following in front of mind:

**'In my belief,
the answer to this question is clearly defined'.**

There are two ways in which you can choose to interpret this statement;
1. how aware are you that the answer to the question is clearly defined
2. for more in-depth analysis you can choose to gather

evidence and confirm the answer to the question. This obviously will take more time, most Self-Assessment users opt for the first way to interpret the question and dig deeper later on based on the outcome of the overall Self-Assessment.

A score of '1' would mean that the answer is not clear at all, where a '5' would mean the answer is crystal clear and defined. Leave emtpy when the question is not applicable or you don't want to answer it, you can skip it without affecting your score. Write your score in the space provided.

After you have responded to all the appropriate statements in each section, compute your average score for that section, using the formula provided, and round to the nearest tenth. Then transfer to the corresponding spoke in the Digital Business Model Scorecard on the second next page of the Self-Assessment.

Your completed Digital Business Model Scorecard will give you a clear presentation of which Digital Business Model areas need attention.

Digital Business Model Scorecard Example

Example of how the finalized Scorecard can look like:

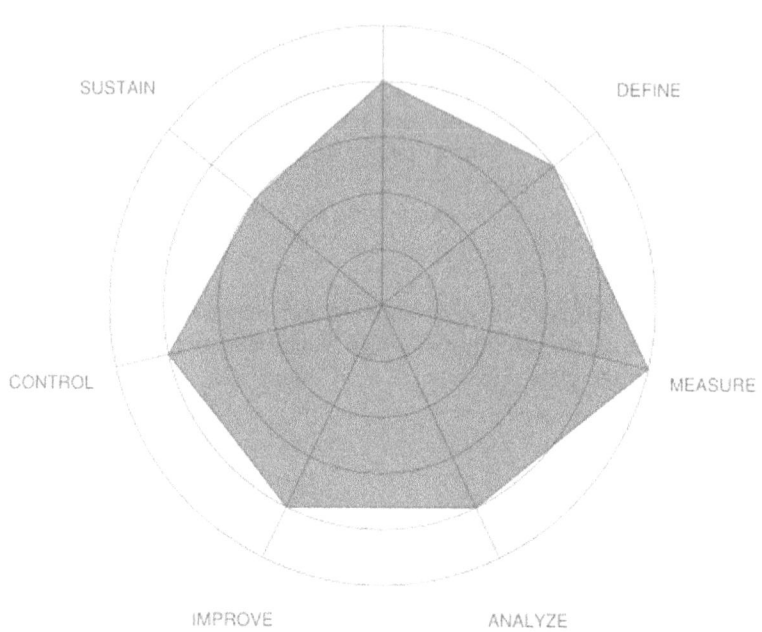

Digital Business Model
Scorecard

Your Scores:

BEGINNING OF THE SELF-ASSESSMENT:

CRITERION #1: RECOGNIZE

INTENT: Be aware of the need for change. Recognize that there is an unfavorable variation, problem or symptom.

In my belief, the answer to this question is clearly defined:

5 Strongly Agree

4 Agree

3 Neutral

2 Disagree

1 Strongly Disagree

1. What are the expected benefits of Digital Business Model to the stakeholder?
<--- Score

2. Is it clear when you think of the day ahead of you what activities and tasks you need to complete?
<--- Score

3. Looking at each person individually – does every

one have the qualities which are needed to work in this group?

<--- Score

4. What situation(s) led to this Digital Business Model Self Assessment?

<--- Score

5. What are the clients issues and concerns?

<--- Score

6. Why the need?

<--- Score

7. Will it solve real problems?

<--- Score

8. Are your goals realistic? Do you need to redefine your problem? Perhaps the problem has changed or maybe you have reached your goal and need to set a new one?

<--- Score

9. What Digital Business Model capabilities do you need?

<--- Score

10. What creative shifts do you need to take?

<--- Score

11. Do you recognize Digital Business Model achievements?

<--- Score

12. What is the smallest subset of the problem you can usefully solve?

<--- Score

13. What is the Digital Business Model problem definition? What do you need to resolve?
<--- Score

14. Is the need for organizational change recognized?
<--- Score

15. Which issues are too important to ignore?
<--- Score

16. Did you miss any major Digital Business Model issues?
<--- Score

17. Where do you need to exercise leadership?
<--- Score

18. What needs to stay?
<--- Score

19. Are employees recognized for desired behaviors?
<--- Score

20. What Digital Business Model coordination do you need?
<--- Score

21. Are there regulatory / compliance issues?
<--- Score

22. How are the Digital Business Model's objectives aligned to the group's overall stakeholder strategy?
<--- Score

23. Will a response program recognize when a crisis occurs and provide some level of response?
<--- Score

24. What Digital Business Model events should you attend?
<--- Score

25. What training and capacity building actions are needed to implement proposed reforms?
<--- Score

26. Who should resolve the Digital Business Model issues?
<--- Score

27. What vendors make products that address the Digital Business Model needs?
<--- Score

28. What information do users need?
<--- Score

29. To what extent would your organization benefit from being recognized as a award recipient?
<--- Score

30. What resources or support might you need?
<--- Score

31. Whom do you really need or want to serve?
<--- Score

32. Which information does the Digital Business Model business case need to include?
<--- Score

33. Who needs to know?
<--- Score

34. How does it fit into your organizational needs and tasks?
<--- Score

35. What are the stakeholder objectives to be achieved with Digital Business Model?
<--- Score

36. Who defines the rules in relation to any given issue?
<--- Score

37. What are the timeframes required to resolve each of the issues/problems?
<--- Score

38. Why is this needed?
<--- Score

39. What needs to be done?
<--- Score

40. How many trainings, in total, are needed?
<--- Score

41. What would happen if Digital Business Model weren't done?
<--- Score

42. What are your needs in relation to Digital Business Model skills, labor, equipment, and markets?
<--- Score

43. As a sponsor, customer or management, how important is it to meet goals, objectives?
<--- Score

44. For your Digital Business Model project, identify and describe the business environment, is there more than one layer to the business environment?
<--- Score

45. What do employees need in the short term?
<--- Score

46. Are there any specific expectations or concerns about the Digital Business Model team, Digital Business Model itself?
<--- Score

47. How much are sponsors, customers, partners, stakeholders involved in Digital Business Model? In other words, what are the risks, if Digital Business Model does not deliver successfully?
<--- Score

48. What else needs to be measured?
<--- Score

49. What activities does the governance board need to consider?
<--- Score

50. Do you have/need 24-hour access to key personnel?
<--- Score

51. What is the problem or issue?

<--- Score

52. Do you need different information or graphics?
<--- Score

53. Are controls defined to recognize and contain problems?
<--- Score

54. Are there recognized Digital Business Model problems?
<--- Score

55. How do you identify the kinds of information that you will need?
<--- Score

56. What does Digital Business Model success mean to the stakeholders?
<--- Score

57. Do you need to avoid or amend any Digital Business Model activities?
<--- Score

58. What problems are you facing and how do you consider Digital Business Model will circumvent those obstacles?
<--- Score

59. Are losses recognized in a timely manner?
<--- Score

60. Are you dealing with any of the same issues today as yesterday? What can you do about this?
<--- Score

61. Does Digital Business Model create potential expectations in other areas that need to be recognized and considered?
<--- Score

62. Who needs budgets?
<--- Score

63. What should be considered when identifying available resources, constraints, and deadlines?
<--- Score

64. Do you know what you need to know about Digital Business Model?
<--- Score

65. Would you recognize a threat from the inside?
<--- Score

66. Consider your own Digital Business Model project, what types of organizational problems do you think might be causing or affecting your problem, based on the work done so far?
<--- Score

67. What do you need to start doing?
<--- Score

68. How do you assess your Digital Business Model workforce capability and capacity needs, including skills, competencies, and staffing levels?
<--- Score

69. What is the recognized need?
<--- Score

70. Does your organization need more Digital Business Model education?
<--- Score

71. What are the Digital Business Model resources needed?
<--- Score

72. Is the quality assurance team identified?
<--- Score

73. Have you identified your Digital Business Model key performance indicators?
<--- Score

74. Is it needed?
<--- Score

75. What is the extent or complexity of the Digital Business Model problem?
<--- Score

76. What extra resources will you need?
<--- Score

77. Who else hopes to benefit from it?
<--- Score

78. Are there Digital Business Model problems defined?
<--- Score

79. What are the minority interests and what amount of minority interests can be recognized?
<--- Score

80. Can management personnel recognize the monetary benefit of Digital Business Model?
<--- Score

81. Are problem definition and motivation clearly presented?
<--- Score

82. How are you going to measure success?
<--- Score

83. Who are your key stakeholders who need to sign off?
<--- Score

84. Where is training needed?
<--- Score

85. How do you take a forward-looking perspective in identifying Digital Business Model research related to market response and models?
<--- Score

86. Are employees recognized or rewarded for performance that demonstrates the highest levels of integrity?
<--- Score

87. When a Digital Business Model manager recognizes a problem, what options are available?
<--- Score

88. How do you identify subcontractor relationships?
<--- Score

89. Who needs what information?
<--- Score

90. What prevents you from making the changes you know will make you a more effective Digital Business Model leader?
<--- Score

91. Are there any revenue recognition issues?
<--- Score

92. Will Digital Business Model deliverables need to be tested and, if so, by whom?
<--- Score

93. What tools and technologies are needed for a custom Digital Business Model project?
<--- Score

Add up total points for this section:
_____ = Total points for this section

Divided by: _____ (number of
statements answered) = _____
Average score for this section

Transfer your score to the Digital Business Model Index at the beginning of the Self-Assessment.

CRITERION #2: DEFINE:

INTENT: Formulate the stakeholder problem. Define the problem, needs and objectives.

In my belief, the answer to this question is clearly defined:

5 Strongly Agree

4 Agree

3 Neutral

2 Disagree

1 Strongly Disagree

1. What is the worst case scenario?
<--- Score

2. Are all requirements met?
<--- Score

3. Has everyone on the team, including the team leaders, been properly trained?
<--- Score

4. What intelligence can you gather?
<--- Score

5. When is/was the Digital Business Model start date?
<--- Score

6. Will team members regularly document their Digital Business Model work?
<--- Score

7. How do you manage scope?
<--- Score

8. What constraints exist that might impact the team?
<--- Score

9. What scope to assess?
<--- Score

10. If substitutes have been appointed, have they been briefed on the Digital Business Model goals and received regular communications as to the progress to date?
<--- Score

11. Is there a clear Digital Business Model case definition?
<--- Score

12. Are customer(s) identified and segmented according to their different needs and requirements?
<--- Score

13. How have you defined all Digital Business Model requirements first?

<--- Score

14. What is the context?
<--- Score

15. How would you define the culture at your organization, how susceptible is it to Digital Business Model changes?
<--- Score

16. Is the team formed and are team leaders (Coaches and Management Leads) assigned?
<--- Score

17. How would you define Digital Business Model leadership?
<--- Score

18. What knowledge or experience is required?
<--- Score

19. Are there any constraints known that bear on the ability to perform Digital Business Model work? How is the team addressing them?
<--- Score

20. How do you catch Digital Business Model definition inconsistencies?
<--- Score

21. Who approved the Digital Business Model scope?
<--- Score

22. Has anyone else (internal or external to the group) attempted to solve this problem or a similar one before? If so, what knowledge can be leveraged from

these previous efforts?
<--- Score

23. What are the boundaries of the scope? What is in bounds and what is not? What is the start point? What is the stop point?
<--- Score

24. Do you all define Digital Business Model in the same way?
<--- Score

25. Is there a completed, verified, and validated high-level 'as is' (not 'should be' or 'could be') stakeholder process map?
<--- Score

26. How do you hand over Digital Business Model context?
<--- Score

27. Is the team adequately staffed with the desired cross-functionality? If not, what additional resources are available to the team?
<--- Score

28. Will a Digital Business Model production readiness review be required?
<--- Score

29. Is scope creep really all bad news?
<--- Score

30. Is the Digital Business Model scope manageable?
<--- Score

31. When is the estimated completion date?
<--- Score

32. Is the current 'as is' process being followed? If not, what are the discrepancies?
<--- Score

33. What Digital Business Model requirements should be gathered?
<--- Score

34. Is there a Digital Business Model management charter, including stakeholder case, problem and goal statements, scope, milestones, roles and responsibilities, communication plan?
<--- Score

35. How often are the team meetings?
<--- Score

36. How do you gather the stories?
<--- Score

37. Who is gathering Digital Business Model information?
<--- Score

38. Has the improvement team collected the 'voice of the customer' (obtained feedback – qualitative and quantitative)?
<--- Score

39. Is the Digital Business Model scope complete and appropriately sized?
<--- Score

40. Is data collected and displayed to better understand customer(s) critical needs and requirements.
<--- Score

41. What is out-of-scope initially?
<--- Score

42. What happens if Digital Business Model's scope changes?
<--- Score

43. Is the work to date meeting requirements?
<--- Score

44. Are the Digital Business Model requirements testable?
<--- Score

45. In what way can you redefine the criteria of choice clients have in your category in your favor?
<--- Score

46. Is Digital Business Model required?
<--- Score

47. Is the improvement team aware of the different versions of a process: what they think it is vs. what it actually is vs. what it should be vs. what it could be?
<--- Score

48. Are task requirements clearly defined?
<--- Score

49. Have specific policy objectives been defined?
<--- Score

50. Has your scope been defined?
<--- Score

51. What is the scope?
<--- Score

52. What is the scope of the Digital Business Model effort?
<--- Score

53. Do the problem and goal statements meet the SMART criteria (specific, measurable, attainable, relevant, and time-bound)?
<--- Score

54. Who are the Digital Business Model improvement team members, including Management Leads and Coaches?
<--- Score

55. Scope of sensitive information?
<--- Score

56. Are audit criteria, scope, frequency and methods defined?
<--- Score

57. What are the requirements for audit information?
<--- Score

58. What are the rough order estimates on cost savings/opportunities that Digital Business Model brings?
<--- Score

59. Is special Digital Business Model user knowledge required?
<--- Score

60. What are the compelling stakeholder reasons for embarking on Digital Business Model?
<--- Score

61. How do you keep key subject matter experts in the loop?
<--- Score

62. Who defines (or who defined) the rules and roles?
<--- Score

63. Are roles and responsibilities formally defined?
<--- Score

64. Is full participation by members in regularly held team meetings guaranteed?
<--- Score

65. Why are you doing Digital Business Model and what is the scope?
<--- Score

66. What specifically is the problem? Where does it occur? When does it occur? What is its extent?
<--- Score

67. What critical content must be communicated – who, what, when, where, and how?
<--- Score

68. Have all of the relationships been defined properly?

<--- Score

69. Do you have a Digital Business Model success story or case study ready to tell and share?
<--- Score

70. What information should you gather?
<--- Score

71. What is the scope of Digital Business Model?
<--- Score

72. What gets examined?
<--- Score

73. Has a Digital Business Model requirement not been met?
<--- Score

74. What is the definition of Digital Business Model excellence?
<--- Score

75. Are resources adequate for the scope?
<--- Score

76. What customer feedback methods were used to solicit their input?
<--- Score

77. Does the scope remain the same?
<--- Score

78. What was the context?
<--- Score

79. Are there different segments of customers?
<--- Score

80. How do you manage unclear Digital Business Model requirements?
<--- Score

81. Are improvement team members fully trained on Digital Business Model?
<--- Score

82. Has/have the customer(s) been identified?
<--- Score

83. Have all basic functions of Digital Business Model been defined?
<--- Score

84. How do you manage changes in Digital Business Model requirements?
<--- Score

85. What is in scope?
<--- Score

86. When are meeting minutes sent out? Who is on the distribution list?
<--- Score

87. Are accountability and ownership for Digital Business Model clearly defined?
<--- Score

88. Are required metrics defined, what are they?
<--- Score

89. Does the team have regular meetings?
<--- Score

90. How can the value of Digital Business Model be defined?
<--- Score

91. Is Digital Business Model linked to key stakeholder goals and objectives?
<--- Score

92. Is there a completed SIPOC representation, describing the Suppliers, Inputs, Process, Outputs, and Customers?
<--- Score

93. Are different versions of process maps needed to account for the different types of inputs?
<--- Score

94. Is the scope of Digital Business Model defined?
<--- Score

95. Will team members perform Digital Business Model work when assigned and in a timely fashion?
<--- Score

96. What are the tasks and definitions?
<--- Score

97. Have the customer needs been translated into specific, measurable requirements? How?
<--- Score

98. What sources do you use to gather information for a Digital Business Model study?

<--- Score

99. Has a project plan, Gantt chart, or similar been developed/completed?
<--- Score

100. What is in the scope and what is not in scope?
<--- Score

101. What are the record-keeping requirements of Digital Business Model activities?
<--- Score

102. What are the Digital Business Model use cases?
<--- Score

103. What are the core elements of the Digital Business Model business case?
<--- Score

104. The political context: who holds power?
<--- Score

105. What defines best in class?
<--- Score

106. How did the Digital Business Model manager receive input to the development of a Digital Business Model improvement plan and the estimated completion dates/times of each activity?
<--- Score

107. What sort of initial information to gather?
<--- Score

108. What are the Roles and Responsibilities for

each team member and its leadership? Where is this documented?
<--- Score

109. What is a worst-case scenario for losses?
<--- Score

110. Is Digital Business Model currently on schedule according to the plan?
<--- Score

111. How was the 'as is' process map developed, reviewed, verified and validated?
<--- Score

112. What are the dynamics of the communication plan?
<--- Score

113. How are consistent Digital Business Model definitions important?
<--- Score

114. Has a high-level 'as is' process map been completed, verified and validated?
<--- Score

115. What system do you use for gathering Digital Business Model information?
<--- Score

116. Is there a critical path to deliver Digital Business Model results?
<--- Score

117. What is the definition of success?

<--- Score

118. How will the Digital Business Model team and the group measure complete success of Digital Business Model?
<--- Score

119. Is there any additional Digital Business Model definition of success?
<--- Score

120. What key stakeholder process output measure(s) does Digital Business Model leverage and how?
<--- Score

121. How will variation in the actual durations of each activity be dealt with to ensure that the expected Digital Business Model results are met?
<--- Score

122. Are stakeholder processes mapped?
<--- Score

123. Has the direction changed at all during the course of Digital Business Model? If so, when did it change and why?
<--- Score

124. Is the team equipped with available and reliable resources?
<--- Score

125. How does the Digital Business Model manager ensure against scope creep?
<--- Score

126. What is out of scope?
<--- Score

127. How do you gather Digital Business Model requirements?
<--- Score

128. How do you gather requirements?
<--- Score

129. Are the Digital Business Model requirements complete?
<--- Score

130. Is there regularly 100% attendance at the team meetings? If not, have appointed substitutes attended to preserve cross-functionality and full representation?
<--- Score

131. Has the Digital Business Model work been fairly and/or equitably divided and delegated among team members who are qualified and capable to perform the work? Has everyone contributed?
<--- Score

132. Is it clearly defined in and to your organization what you do?
<--- Score

133. What would be the goal or target for a Digital Business Model's improvement team?
<--- Score

134. How is the team tracking and documenting its work?

<--- Score

135. What are (control) requirements for Digital
Business Model Information?
<--- Score

136. Is the team sponsored by a champion or
stakeholder leader?
<--- Score

137. Are approval levels defined for contracts and
supplements to contracts?
<--- Score

138. How and when will the baselines be defined?
<--- Score

139. What Digital Business Model services do you
require?
<--- Score

140. Has a team charter been developed and
communicated?
<--- Score

141. Do you have organizational privacy
requirements?
<--- Score

142. What are the Digital Business Model tasks and
definitions?
<--- Score

Add up total points for this section:
_ _ _ _ _ = Total points for this section

Divided by: _____ (number of
statements answered) = _____
Average score for this section

Transfer your score to the Digital
Business Model Index at the beginning
of the Self-Assessment.

CRITERION #3: MEASURE:

INTENT: Gather the correct data.
Measure the current performance and
evolution of the situation.

In my belief, the answer to this
question is clearly defined:

5 Strongly Agree

4 Agree

3 Neutral

2 Disagree

1 Strongly Disagree

1. What are your customers expectations and measures?
<--- Score

2. Are Digital Business Model vulnerabilities categorized and prioritized?
<--- Score

3. How are costs allocated?

<--- Score

4. Among the Digital Business Model product and service cost to be estimated, which is considered hardest to estimate?
<--- Score

5. What drives O&M cost?
<--- Score

6. Is it possible to estimate the impact of unanticipated complexity such as wrong or failed assumptions, feedback, etcetera on proposed reforms?
<--- Score

7. What are your operating costs?
<--- Score

8. Are actual costs in line with budgeted costs?
<--- Score

9. How do you measure efficient delivery of Digital Business Model services?
<--- Score

10. Have you included everything in your Digital Business Model cost models?
<--- Score

11. What is the total cost related to deploying Digital Business Model, including any consulting or professional services?
<--- Score

12. How do you measure variability?

<--- Score

13. Are you taking your company in the direction of better and revenue or cheaper and cost?
<--- Score

14. What are your key Digital Business Model organizational performance measures, including key short and longer-term financial measures?
<--- Score

15. What does losing customers cost your organization?
<--- Score

16. What details are required of the Digital Business Model cost structure?
<--- Score

17. What are hidden Digital Business Model quality costs?
<--- Score

18. How can you reduce costs?
<--- Score

19. Do you have a flow diagram of what happens?
<--- Score

20. How do you verify the authenticity of the data and information used?
<--- Score

21. How do you control the overall costs of your work processes?
<--- Score

22. How do you verify performance?
<--- Score

23. Did you tackle the cause or the symptom?
<--- Score

24. What measurements are possible, practicable and meaningful?
<--- Score

25. Are there any easy-to-implement alternatives to Digital Business Model? Sometimes other solutions are available that do not require the cost implications of a full-blown project?
<--- Score

26. How do you measure success?
<--- Score

27. How will effects be measured?
<--- Score

28. Do you aggressively reward and promote the people who have the biggest impact on creating excellent Digital Business Model services/products?
<--- Score

29. When a disaster occurs, who gets priority?
<--- Score

30. What are the current costs of the Digital Business Model process?
<--- Score

31. At what cost?

<--- Score

32. How are measurements made?
<--- Score

33. What does a Test Case verify?
<--- Score

34. Have you made assumptions about the shape of the future, particularly its impact on your customers and competitors?
<--- Score

35. Is the solution cost-effective?
<--- Score

36. Has a cost center been established?
<--- Score

37. What are the Digital Business Model investment costs?
<--- Score

38. How will you measure your Digital Business Model effectiveness?
<--- Score

39. What users will be impacted?
<--- Score

40. What is your Digital Business Model quality cost segregation study?
<--- Score

41. What evidence is there and what is measured?
<--- Score

42. How can you manage cost down?
<--- Score

43. What are the costs?
<--- Score

44. How is the value delivered by Digital Business Model being measured?
<--- Score

45. What are your primary costs, revenues, assets?
<--- Score

46. What disadvantage does this cause for the user?
<--- Score

47. Are you aware of what could cause a problem?
<--- Score

48. What causes mismanagement?
<--- Score

49. What causes investor action?
<--- Score

50. What potential environmental factors impact the Digital Business Model effort?
<--- Score

51. What is the Digital Business Model business impact?
<--- Score

52. How is progress measured?
<--- Score

53. Does the Digital Business Model task fit the client's priorities?
<--- Score

54. What are the types and number of measures to use?
<--- Score

55. What relevant entities could be measured?
<--- Score

56. How to cause the change?
<--- Score

57. When should you bother with diagrams?
<--- Score

58. Who should receive measurement reports?
<--- Score

59. What are the uncertainties surrounding estimates of impact?
<--- Score

60. What is the total fixed cost?
<--- Score

61. Are the units of measure consistent?
<--- Score

62. What are the costs of delaying Digital Business Model action?
<--- Score

63. Does management have the right priorities

among projects?
<--- Score

64. What methods are feasible and acceptable to estimate the impact of reforms?
<--- Score

65. How will your organization measure success?
<--- Score

66. How do you aggregate measures across priorities?
<--- Score

67. What is the root cause(s) of the problem?
<--- Score

68. What measurements are being captured?
<--- Score

69. What do you measure and why?
<--- Score

70. How do you measure lifecycle phases?
<--- Score

71. When are costs are incurred?
<--- Score

72. How can you measure Digital Business Model in a systematic way?
<--- Score

73. How do you verify your resources?
<--- Score

74. Do you have any cost Digital Business Model

limitation requirements?
<--- Score

75. Is the cost worth the Digital Business Model effort
?
<--- Score

76. What is the cost of rework?
<--- Score

77. Are the measurements objective?
<--- Score

78. Are there competing Digital Business Model
priorities?
<--- Score

79. How do your measurements capture actionable
Digital Business Model information for use in
exceeding your customers expectations and securing
your customers engagement?
<--- Score

80. What is an unallowable cost?
<--- Score

81. How can a Digital Business Model test verify your
ideas or assumptions?
<--- Score

82. What are the operational costs after Digital
Business Model deployment?
<--- Score

83. Are there measurements based on task
performance?

<--- Score

84. Why do the measurements/indicators matter?
<--- Score

85. How long to keep data and how to manage retention costs?
<--- Score

86. Will Digital Business Model have an impact on current business continuity, disaster recovery processes and/or infrastructure?
<--- Score

87. Have design-to-cost goals been established?
<--- Score

88. What tests verify requirements?
<--- Score

89. How will success or failure be measured?
<--- Score

90. Do the benefits outweigh the costs?
<--- Score

91. What could cause delays in the schedule?
<--- Score

92. Does a Digital Business Model quantification method exist?
<--- Score

93. Is there an opportunity to verify requirements?
<--- Score

94. What would be a real cause for concern?
<--- Score

95. What harm might be caused?
<--- Score

96. Which measures and indicators matter?
<--- Score

97. How do you verify and develop ideas and innovations?
<--- Score

98. Are supply costs steady or fluctuating?
<--- Score

99. What do people want to verify?
<--- Score

100. How frequently do you track Digital Business Model measures?
<--- Score

101. How will measures be used to manage and adapt?
<--- Score

102. What causes extra work or rework?
<--- Score

103. Over the next three years, how much of a priority will the shift to a digital business model be for your organization?
<--- Score

104. Are missed Digital Business Model opportunities

costing your organization money?
<--- Score

105. What is measured? Why?
<--- Score

106. What are allowable costs?
<--- Score

107. How can you reduce the costs of obtaining inputs?
<--- Score

108. Are you able to realize any cost savings?
<--- Score

109. What can be used to verify compliance?
<--- Score

110. What are the costs of reform?
<--- Score

111. Are indirect costs charged to the Digital Business Model program?
<--- Score

112. Which Digital Business Model impacts are significant?
<--- Score

113. Do you have an issue in getting priority?
<--- Score

114. What would it cost to replace your technology?
<--- Score

115. Was a business case (cost/benefit) developed?
<--- Score

116. What are the estimated costs of proposed changes?
<--- Score

117. Where is the cost?
<--- Score

118. How will costs be allocated?
<--- Score

119. Security vendors - what is the impact of digital business models on security strategies?
<--- Score

120. Do you effectively measure and reward individual and team performance?
<--- Score

121. What are the Digital Business Model key cost drivers?
<--- Score

122. How will you measure success?
<--- Score

123. Where is it measured?
<--- Score

124. How do you quantify and qualify impacts?
<--- Score

125. What is your decision requirements diagram?
<--- Score

126. How much does it cost?
<--- Score

127. How do you verify the Digital Business Model requirements quality?
<--- Score

128. How can you measure the performance?
<--- Score

129. What are the costs and benefits?
<--- Score

130. What does your operating model cost?
<--- Score

Add up total points for this section:
_ _ _ _ _ = Total points for this section

Divided by: _ _ _ _ _ _ (number of statements answered) = _ _ _ _ _ _
Average score for this section

Transfer your score to the Digital Business Model Index at the beginning of the Self-Assessment.

CRITERION #4: ANALYZE:

INTENT: Analyze causes, assumptions and hypotheses.

In my belief, the answer to this question is clearly defined:

5 Strongly Agree

4 Agree

3 Neutral

2 Disagree

1 Strongly Disagree

1. How much data can be collected in the given timeframe?
<--- Score

2. How often will data be collected for measures?
<--- Score

3. How many input/output points does it require?
<--- Score

4. Who is involved in the management review process?
<--- Score

5. How is the data gathered?
<--- Score

6. Who gets your output?
<--- Score

7. What types of data do your Digital Business Model indicators require?
<--- Score

8. What are your current levels and trends in key Digital Business Model measures or indicators of product and process performance that are important to and directly serve your customers?
<--- Score

9. What controls do you have in place to protect data?
<--- Score

10. Do your leaders quickly bounce back from setbacks?
<--- Score

11. Were there any improvement opportunities identified from the process analysis?
<--- Score

12. What tools were used to narrow the list of possible causes?
<--- Score

13. Are all team members qualified for all tasks?

<--- Score

14. Where can you get qualified talent today?
<--- Score

15. What are the best opportunities for value improvement?
<--- Score

16. Was a cause-and-effect diagram used to explore the different types of causes (or sources of variation)?
<--- Score

17. What, related to, Digital Business Model processes does your organization outsource?
<--- Score

18. What qualifications and skills do you need?
<--- Score

19. Do several people in different organizational units assist with the Digital Business Model process?
<--- Score

20. Should you invest in industry-recognized qualifications?
<--- Score

21. What does the data say about the performance of the stakeholder process?
<--- Score

22. How do you use Digital Business Model data and information to support organizational decision making and innovation?
<--- Score

23. Think about the functions involved in your Digital Business Model project, what processes flow from these functions?
<--- Score

24. How is the Digital Business Model Value Stream Mapping managed?
<--- Score

25. Has an output goal been set?
<--- Score

26. A compounding model resolution with available relevant data can often provide insight towards a solution methodology; which Digital Business Model models, tools and techniques are necessary?
<--- Score

27. How do you define collaboration and team output?
<--- Score

28. Who qualifies to gain access to data?
<--- Score

29. What are your Digital Business Model processes?
<--- Score

30. How has the Digital Business Model data been gathered?
<--- Score

31. How do you ensure that the Digital Business Model opportunity is realistic?
<--- Score

32. What is the Digital Business Model Driver?
<--- Score

33. How are outputs preserved and protected?
<--- Score

34. What is your organizations process which leads to recognition of value generation?
<--- Score

35. Where is the data coming from to measure compliance?
<--- Score

36. Are your outputs consistent?
<--- Score

37. How do you implement and manage your work processes to ensure that they meet design requirements?
<--- Score

38. Is there a strict change management process?
<--- Score

39. How will the change process be managed?
<--- Score

40. An organizationally feasible system request is one that considers the mission, goals and objectives of the organization, key questions are: is the Digital Business Model solution request practical and will it solve a problem or take advantage of an opportunity to achieve company goals?
<--- Score

41. What is the oversight process?
<--- Score

42. What were the financial benefits resulting from any 'ground fruit or low-hanging fruit' (quick fixes)?
<--- Score

43. Who will gather what data?
<--- Score

44. What are the revised rough estimates of the financial savings/opportunity for Digital Business Model improvements?
<--- Score

45. What data do you need to collect?
<--- Score

46. How can risk management be tied procedurally to process elements?
<--- Score

47. Has data output been validated?
<--- Score

48. Is the required Digital Business Model data gathered?
<--- Score

49. How do your work systems and key work processes relate to and capitalize on your core competencies?
<--- Score

50. What will drive Digital Business Model change?

<--- Score

51. What Digital Business Model data do you gather or use now?
<--- Score

52. What are the personnel training and qualifications required?
<--- Score

53. What data is gathered?
<--- Score

54. Have you defined which data is gathered how?
<--- Score

55. Is there an established change management process?
<--- Score

56. What is the Value Stream Mapping?
<--- Score

57. How do you identify specific Digital Business Model investment opportunities and emerging trends?
<--- Score

58. Were any designed experiments used to generate additional insight into the data analysis?
<--- Score

59. How will the Digital Business Model data be captured?
<--- Score

60. What were the crucial 'moments of truth' on the process map?
<--- Score

61. What methods do you use to gather Digital Business Model data?
<--- Score

62. Where is Digital Business Model data gathered?
<--- Score

63. How do you promote understanding that opportunity for improvement is not criticism of the status quo, or the people who created the status quo?
<--- Score

64. Is pre-qualification of suppliers carried out?
<--- Score

65. How is the way you as the leader think and process information affecting your organizational culture?
<--- Score

66. What process improvements will be needed?
<--- Score

67. Was a detailed process map created to amplify critical steps of the 'as is' stakeholder process?
<--- Score

68. Can you add value to the current Digital Business Model decision-making process (largely qualitative) by incorporating uncertainty modeling (more quantitative)?
<--- Score

69. What Digital Business Model data should be collected?
<--- Score

70. What qualifications do Digital Business Model leaders need?
<--- Score

71. How do you measure the operational performance of your key work systems and processes, including productivity, cycle time, and other appropriate measures of process effectiveness, efficiency, and innovation?
<--- Score

72. How difficult is it to qualify what Digital Business Model ROI is?
<--- Score

73. What is the complexity of the output produced?
<--- Score

74. How does the organization define, manage, and improve its Digital Business Model processes?
<--- Score

75. What other jobs or tasks affect the performance of the steps in the Digital Business Model process?
<--- Score

76. What internal processes need improvement?
<--- Score

77. Do staff qualifications match your project?
<--- Score

78. What process should you select for improvement?
<--- Score

79. What are your current levels and trends in key measures or indicators of Digital Business Model product and process performance that are important to and directly serve your customers? How do these results compare with the performance of your competitors and other organizations with similar offerings?
<--- Score

80. What systems/processes must you excel at?
<--- Score

81. What qualifications are needed?
<--- Score

82. Record-keeping requirements flow from the records needed as inputs, outputs, controls and for transformation of a Digital Business Model process, are the records needed as inputs to the Digital Business Model process available?
<--- Score

83. Which Digital Business Model data should be retained?
<--- Score

84. What Digital Business Model data should be managed?
<--- Score

85. How do mission and objectives affect the Digital Business Model processes of your organization?
<--- Score

86. What are the Digital Business Model design outputs?

<--- Score

87. Who will facilitate the team and process?

<--- Score

88. Do your contracts/agreements contain data security obligations?

<--- Score

89. What Digital Business Model data will be collected?

<--- Score

90. Were Pareto charts (or similar) used to portray the 'heavy hitters' (or key sources of variation)?

<--- Score

91. What are the Digital Business Model business drivers?

<--- Score

92. What training and qualifications will you need?

<--- Score

93. Are you missing Digital Business Model opportunities?

<--- Score

94. What conclusions were drawn from the team's data collection and analysis? How did the team reach these conclusions?

<--- Score

95. What resources go in to get the desired output?
<--- Score

96. What is your organizations system for selecting qualified vendors?
<--- Score

97. What are the necessary qualifications?
<--- Score

98. Do you have the authority to produce the output?
<--- Score

99. Do you, as a leader, bounce back quickly from setbacks?
<--- Score

100. What kind of crime could a potential new hire have committed that would not only not disqualify him/her from being hired by your organization, but would actually indicate that he/she might be a particularly good fit?
<--- Score

101. What are the processes for audit reporting and management?
<--- Score

102. How will the data be checked for quality?
<--- Score

103. What are your key performance measures or indicators and in-process measures for the control and improvement of your Digital Business Model processes?
<--- Score

104. What qualifications are necessary?
<--- Score

105. Do you understand your management processes today?
<--- Score

106. Who is involved with workflow mapping?
<--- Score

107. Do quality systems drive continuous improvement?
<--- Score

108. Are all staff in core Digital Business Model subjects Highly Qualified?
<--- Score

109. What are evaluation criteria for the output?
<--- Score

110. What output to create?
<--- Score

111. Is there any way to speed up the process?
<--- Score

112. What Digital Business Model metrics are outputs of the process?
<--- Score

113. What successful thing are you doing today that may be blinding you to new growth opportunities?
<--- Score

114. What did the team gain from developing a sub-process map?
<--- Score

115. What other organizational variables, such as reward systems or communication systems, affect the performance of this Digital Business Model process?
<--- Score

116. What do you need to qualify?
<--- Score

117. What qualifies as competition?
<--- Score

118. What information qualified as important?
<--- Score

119. What is the cost of poor quality as supported by the team's analysis?
<--- Score

120. Is the final output clearly identified?
<--- Score

121. Do your employees have the opportunity to do what they do best everyday?
<--- Score

122. How is data used for program management and improvement?
<--- Score

123. When should a process be art not science?
<--- Score

124. What are the disruptive Digital Business Model technologies that enable your organization to radically change your business processes?
<--- Score

125. Are Digital Business Model changes recognized early enough to be approved through the regular process?
<--- Score

126. Identify an operational issue in your organization, for example, could a particular task be done more quickly or more efficiently by Digital Business Model?
<--- Score

127. Think about some of the processes you undertake within your organization, which do you own?
<--- Score

128. Is the suppliers process defined and controlled?
<--- Score

129. How will corresponding data be collected?
<--- Score

130. Who owns what data?
<--- Score

131. What tools were used to generate the list of possible causes?
<--- Score

132. What quality tools were used to get through the analyze phase?
<--- Score

133. What are your outputs?
<--- Score

Add up total points for this section:
_ _ _ _ _ = Total points for this section

Divided by: _ _ _ _ _ _ (number of
statements answered) = _ _ _ _ _ _
Average score for this section

Transfer your score to the Digital
Business Model Index at the beginning
of the Self-Assessment.

CRITERION #5: IMPROVE:

INTENT: Develop a practical solution. Innovate, establish and test the solution and to measure the results.

In my belief, the answer to this question is clearly defined:

5 Strongly Agree

4 Agree

3 Neutral

2 Disagree

1 Strongly Disagree

1. Who will be responsible for documenting the Digital Business Model requirements in detail?
<--- Score

2. What tools do you use once you have decided on a Digital Business Model strategy and more importantly how do you choose?
<--- Score

3. How do you deal with Digital Business Model risk?
<--- Score

4. Have you achieved Digital Business Model improvements?
<--- Score

5. Who will be using the results of the measurement activities?
<--- Score

6. To what extent does management recognize Digital Business Model as a tool to increase the results?
<--- Score

7. Are you assessing Digital Business Model and risk?
<--- Score

8. What is the implementation plan?
<--- Score

9. What tools were most useful during the improve phase?
<--- Score

10. What lessons, if any, from a pilot were incorporated into the design of the full-scale solution?
<--- Score

11. In the past few months, what is the smallest change you have made that has had the biggest positive result? What was it about that small change that produced the large return?
<--- Score

12. Do those selected for the Digital Business Model

team have a good general understanding of what
Digital Business Model is all about?
<--- Score

13. Is there any other Digital Business Model solution?
<--- Score

14. Where do the Digital Business Model decisions
reside?
<--- Score

15. How do you improve productivity?
<--- Score

16. How can skill-level changes improve Digital
Business Model?
<--- Score

17. How do the Digital Business Model results
compare with the performance of your competitors
and other organizations with similar offerings?
<--- Score

18. How will you recognize and celebrate results?
<--- Score

19. How do you measure risk?
<--- Score

**20. How can you develop an effective digital
business model?**
<--- Score

21. Why improve in the first place?
<--- Score

22. What were the underlying assumptions on the cost-benefit analysis?
<--- Score

23. How will you know that you have improved?
<--- Score

24. What practices helps your organization to develop its capacity to recognize patterns?
<--- Score

25. What is Digital Business Model's impact on utilizing the best solution(s)?
<--- Score

26. How will you measure the results?
<--- Score

27. Is the Digital Business Model risk managed?
<--- Score

28. How does your organization evaluate strategic Digital Business Model success?
<--- Score

29. Risk factors: what are the characteristics of Digital Business Model that make it risky?
<--- Score

30. Which of the recognised risks out of all risks can be most likely transferred?
<--- Score

31. For decision problems, how do you develop a decision statement?
<--- Score

32. Is supporting Digital Business Model documentation required?
<--- Score

33. How do you measure progress and evaluate training effectiveness?
<--- Score

34. Does a good decision guarantee a good outcome?
<--- Score

35. What alternative responses are available to manage risk?
<--- Score

36. Who should make the Digital Business Model decisions?
<--- Score

37. Would you develop a Digital Business Model Communication Strategy?
<--- Score

38. What to do with the results or outcomes of measurements?
<--- Score

39. Who manages Digital Business Model risk?
<--- Score

40. What are the implications of the one critical Digital Business Model decision 10 minutes, 10 months, and 10 years from now?
<--- Score

41. Do vendor agreements bring new compliance risk ?

<--- Score

42. Will the controls trigger any other risks?

<--- Score

43. What does the 'should be' process map/design look like?

<--- Score

44. Have you identified breakpoints and/or risk tolerances that will trigger broad consideration of a potential need for intervention or modification of strategy?

<--- Score

45. For estimation problems, how do you develop an estimation statement?

<--- Score

46. How do you manage Digital Business Model risk?

<--- Score

47. Is the scope clearly documented?

<--- Score

48. Were any criteria developed to assist the team in testing and evaluating potential solutions?

<--- Score

49. What are your current levels and trends in key measures or indicators of workforce and leader development?

<--- Score

50. How significant is the improvement in the eyes of the end user?
<--- Score

51. Explorations of the frontiers of Digital Business Model will help you build influence, improve Digital Business Model, optimize decision making, and sustain change, what is your approach?
<--- Score

52. Are the key business and technology risks being managed?
<--- Score

53. How can you improve performance?
<--- Score

54. What is Digital Business Model risk?
<--- Score

55. What were the criteria for evaluating a Digital Business Model pilot?
<--- Score

56. What assumptions are made about the solution and approach?
<--- Score

57. How will you know that a change is an improvement?
<--- Score

58. How risky is your organization?
<--- Score

59. Is the Digital Business Model solution sustainable?

<--- Score

60. What can you do to improve?
<--- Score

61. Is the Digital Business Model documentation thorough?
<--- Score

62. How do you mitigate Digital Business Model risk?
<--- Score

63. How can you improve Digital Business Model?
<--- Score

64. What criteria will you use to assess your Digital Business Model risks?
<--- Score

65. What strategies for Digital Business Model improvement are successful?
<--- Score

66. Who will be responsible for making the decisions to include or exclude requested changes once Digital Business Model is underway?
<--- Score

67. What is the risk?
<--- Score

68. Who do you report Digital Business Model results to?
<--- Score

69. How are Digital Business Model risks managed?

<--- Score

70. Are risk management tasks balanced centrally and locally?
<--- Score

71. Risk Identification: What are the possible risk events your organization faces in relation to Digital Business Model?
<--- Score

72. Is any Digital Business Model documentation required?
<--- Score

73. How can the phases of Digital Business Model development be identified?
<--- Score

74. If you could go back in time five years, what decision would you make differently? What is your best guess as to what decision you're making today you might regret five years from now?
<--- Score

75. Is risk periodically assessed?
<--- Score

76. What error proofing will be done to address some of the discrepancies observed in the 'as is' process?
<--- Score

77. Are decisions made in a timely manner?
<--- Score

78. Digital Business Model risk decisions: whose call Is

It?
<--- Score

79. How scalable is your Digital Business Model solution?
<--- Score

80. What improvements have been achieved?
<--- Score

81. What is the magnitude of the improvements?
<--- Score

82. Who are the Digital Business Model decision makers?
<--- Score

83. What attendant changes will need to be made to ensure that the solution is successful?
<--- Score

84. How do you go about comparing Digital Business Model approaches/solutions?
<--- Score

85. How is knowledge sharing about risk management improved?
<--- Score

86. How will you know when its improved?
<--- Score

87. What do you want to improve?
<--- Score

88. How are policy decisions made and where?

<--- Score

89. How is continuous improvement applied to risk management?
<--- Score

90. Are the most efficient solutions problem-specific?
<--- Score

91. Is the measure of success for Digital Business Model understandable to a variety of people?
<--- Score

92. Can the solution be designed and implemented within an acceptable time period?
<--- Score

93. Do you have the optimal project management team structure?
<--- Score

94. Who controls the risk?
<--- Score

95. Does the goal represent a desired result that can be measured?
<--- Score

96. What needs improvement? Why?
<--- Score

97. Are events managed to resolution?
<--- Score

98. Who are the key stakeholders for the Digital Business Model evaluation?

<--- Score

99. What tools were used to evaluate the potential solutions?
<--- Score

100. What current systems have to be understood and/or changed?
<--- Score

101. Who are the people involved in developing and implementing Digital Business Model?
<--- Score

102. What resources are required for the improvement efforts?
<--- Score

103. What communications are necessary to support the implementation of the solution?
<--- Score

104. How do you decide how much to remunerate an employee?
<--- Score

105. Do you combine technical expertise with business knowledge and Digital Business Model Key topics include lifecycles, development approaches, requirements and how to make a business case?
<--- Score

106. Are risk triggers captured?
<--- Score

107. What is the team's contingency plan for potential

problems occurring in implementation?
<--- Score

108. What Digital Business Model improvements can be made?
<--- Score

109. Can you identify any significant risks or exposures to Digital Business Model third- parties (vendors, service providers, alliance partners etc) that concern you?
<--- Score

110. Are procedures documented for managing Digital Business Model risks?
<--- Score

111. Can you integrate quality management and risk management?
<--- Score

112. How does the team improve its work?
<--- Score

113. What should a proof of concept or pilot accomplish?
<--- Score

114. What actually has to improve and by how much?
<--- Score

115. What are the Digital Business Model security risks?
<--- Score

116. What tools were used to tap into the creativity

and encourage 'outside the box' thinking?
<--- Score

117. Is there a high likelihood that any
recommendations will achieve their intended results?
<--- Score

118. Is Digital Business Model documentation
maintained?
<--- Score

119. Risk events: what are the things that could go
wrong?
<--- Score

120. Who makes the Digital Business Model decisions
in your organization?
<--- Score

121. How do you manage and improve your Digital
Business Model work systems to deliver customer
value and achieve organizational success and
sustainability?
<--- Score

122. Who manages supplier risk management in your
organization?
<--- Score

123. How do you define the solutions' scope?
<--- Score

124. Do you need to do a usability evaluation?
<--- Score

125. How do you link measurement and risk?

<--- Score

126. Which Digital Business Model solution is appropriate?
<--- Score

127. Was a Digital Business Model charter developed?
<--- Score

128. When you map the key players in your own work and the types/domains of relationships with them, which relationships do you find easy and which challenging, and why?
<--- Score

129. Are the risks fully understood, reasonable and manageable?
<--- Score

130. What risks do you need to manage?
<--- Score

131. How can you better manage risk?
<--- Score

132. How do you measure improved Digital Business Model service perception, and satisfaction?
<--- Score

133. How do you keep improving Digital Business Model?
<--- Score

134. Who are the Digital Business Model decision-makers?
<--- Score

135. What are the concrete Digital Business Model results?
<--- Score

Add up total points for this section:
_ _ _ _ _ = Total points for this section

Divided by: _ _ _ _ _ _ _ (number of
statements answered) = _ _ _ _ _ _
Average score for this section

Transfer your score to the Digital
Business Model Index at the beginning
of the Self-Assessment.

CRITERION #6: CONTROL:

INTENT: Implement the practical solution. Maintain the performance and correct possible complications.

In my belief, the answer to this question is clearly defined:

5 Strongly Agree

4 Agree

3 Neutral

2 Disagree

1 Strongly Disagree

1. Has the improved process and its steps been standardized?
<--- Score

2. Who will be in control?
<--- Score

3. Will existing staff require re-training, for example, to learn new business processes?

<--- Score

4. Does job training on the documented procedures need to be part of the process team's education and training?
<--- Score

5. Will any special training be provided for results interpretation?
<--- Score

6. What adjustments to the strategies are needed?
<--- Score

7. How do you select, collect, align, and integrate Digital Business Model data and information for tracking daily operations and overall organizational performance, including progress relative to strategic objectives and action plans?
<--- Score

8. How do senior leaders actions reflect a commitment to the organizations Digital Business Model values?
<--- Score

9. Do you monitor the Digital Business Model decisions made and fine tune them as they evolve?
<--- Score

10. What are the critical parameters to watch?
<--- Score

11. Is there a recommended audit plan for routine surveillance inspections of Digital Business Model's gains?

<--- Score

12. Who is going to spread your message?
<--- Score

13. What can you control?
<--- Score

14. How can you best use all of your knowledge repositories to enhance learning and sharing?
<--- Score

15. How will the process owner verify improvement in present and future sigma levels, process capabilities?
<--- Score

16. How widespread is its use?
<--- Score

17. How is change control managed?
<--- Score

18. What are the performance and scale of the Digital Business Model tools?
<--- Score

19. Who is the Digital Business Model process owner?
<--- Score

20. What other areas of the group might benefit from the Digital Business Model team's improvements, knowledge, and learning?
<--- Score

21. How do you establish and deploy modified action plans if circumstances require a shift in plans and

rapid execution of new plans?

<--- Score

22. What are the key elements of your Digital Business Model performance improvement system, including your evaluation, organizational learning, and innovation processes?

<--- Score

23. Are there documented procedures?

<--- Score

24. Does the response plan contain a definite closed loop continual improvement scheme (e.g., plan-do-check-act)?

<--- Score

25. Are controls in place and consistently applied?

<--- Score

26. Is there a control plan in place for sustaining improvements (short and long-term)?

<--- Score

27. Can you adapt and adjust to changing Digital Business Model situations?

<--- Score

28. How do you spread information?

<--- Score

29. What is the control/monitoring plan?

<--- Score

30. Have new or revised work instructions resulted?

<--- Score

31. Act/Adjust: What Do you Need to Do Differently?
<--- Score

32. Are documented procedures clear and easy to follow for the operators?
<--- Score

33. Who has control over resources?
<--- Score

34. Is the Digital Business Model test/monitoring cost justified?
<--- Score

35. Do the Digital Business Model decisions you make today help people and the planet tomorrow?
<--- Score

36. How do you monitor usage and cost?
<--- Score

37. Who controls critical resources?
<--- Score

38. Is a response plan established and deployed?
<--- Score

39. Will the team be available to assist members in planning investigations?
<--- Score

40. Are the Digital Business Model standards challenging?
<--- Score

41. How will Digital Business Model decisions be made and monitored?

<--- Score

42. How do you encourage people to take control and responsibility?

<--- Score

43. In the case of a Digital Business Model project, the criteria for the audit derive from implementation objectives, an audit of a Digital Business Model project involves assessing whether the recommendations outlined for implementation have been met, can you track that any Digital Business Model project is implemented as planned, and is it working?

<--- Score

44. How will the process owner and team be able to hold the gains?

<--- Score

45. Does the Digital Business Model performance meet the customer's requirements?

<--- Score

46. Do you monitor the effectiveness of your Digital Business Model activities?

<--- Score

47. What should you measure to verify efficiency gains?

<--- Score

48. What key inputs and outputs are being measured on an ongoing basis?

<--- Score

49. Do the viable solutions scale to future needs?
<--- Score

50. How likely is the current Digital Business Model plan to come in on schedule or on budget?
<--- Score

51. Is there a standardized process?
<--- Score

52. What is the best design framework for Digital Business Model organization now that, in a post industrial-age if the top-down, command and control model is no longer relevant?
<--- Score

53. Is there an action plan in case of emergencies?
<--- Score

54. Is there documentation that will support the successful operation of the improvement?
<--- Score

55. Are the planned controls working?
<--- Score

56. What Digital Business Model standards are applicable?
<--- Score

57. How will report readings be checked to effectively monitor performance?
<--- Score

58. How do controls support value?
<--- Score

59. Are pertinent alerts monitored, analyzed and distributed to appropriate personnel?
<--- Score

60. What is your plan to assess your security risks?
<--- Score

61. Has the Digital Business Model value of standards been quantified?
<--- Score

62. What quality tools were useful in the control phase?
<--- Score

63. Is there a transfer of ownership and knowledge to process owner and process team tasked with the responsibilities.
<--- Score

64. Are the planned controls in place?
<--- Score

65. What is your theory of human motivation, and how does your compensation plan fit with that view?
<--- Score

66. Will your goals reflect your program budget?
<--- Score

67. What other systems, operations, processes, and infrastructures (hiring practices, staffing, training, incentives/rewards, metrics/dashboards/scorecards,

etc.) need updates, additions, changes, or deletions in order to facilitate knowledge transfer and improvements?
<--- Score

68. Are suggested corrective/restorative actions indicated on the response plan for known causes to problems that might surface?
<--- Score

69. How is Digital Business Model project cost planned, managed, monitored?
<--- Score

70. What do your reports reflect?
<--- Score

71. What are customers monitoring?
<--- Score

72. What do you stand for--and what are you against?
<--- Score

73. Are you measuring, monitoring and predicting Digital Business Model activities to optimize operations and profitability, and enhancing outcomes?
<--- Score

74. How will new or emerging customer needs/ requirements be checked/communicated to orient the process toward meeting the new specifications and continually reducing variation?
<--- Score

75. How will you measure your QA plan's

effectiveness?

<--- Score

76. Is there a Digital Business Model Communication plan covering who needs to get what information when?

<--- Score

77. What can procure-to-pay learn from digital business models?

<--- Score

78. What are you attempting to measure/monitor?

<--- Score

79. Is reporting being used or needed?

<--- Score

80. What is the recommended frequency of auditing?

<--- Score

81. What are the known security controls?

<--- Score

82. Are new process steps, standards, and documentation ingrained into normal operations?

<--- Score

83. How do you plan for the cost of succession?

<--- Score

84. You may have created your quality measures at a time when you lacked resources, technology wasn't up to the required standard, or low service levels were the industry norm. Have those circumstances changed?

<--- Score

85. Does a troubleshooting guide exist or is it needed?
<--- Score

86. Is knowledge gained on process shared and institutionalized?
<--- Score

87. How might the group capture best practices and lessons learned so as to leverage improvements?
<--- Score

88. Where do ideas that reach policy makers and planners as proposals for Digital Business Model strengthening and reform actually originate?
<--- Score

89. Against what alternative is success being measured?
<--- Score

90. Can support from partners be adjusted?
<--- Score

91. Does Digital Business Model appropriately measure and monitor risk?
<--- Score

92. Are operating procedures consistent?
<--- Score

93. What is the standard for acceptable Digital Business Model performance?
<--- Score

94. Is there a documented and implemented monitoring plan?
<--- Score

95. What do you measure to verify effectiveness gains?
<--- Score

96. What are your results for key measures or indicators of the accomplishment of your Digital Business Model strategy and action plans, including building and strengthening core competencies?
<--- Score

97. What should the next improvement project be that is related to Digital Business Model?
<--- Score

98. Is a response plan in place for when the input, process, or output measures indicate an 'out-of-control' condition?
<--- Score

99. Is new knowledge gained imbedded in the response plan?
<--- Score

100. How will input, process, and output variables be checked to detect for sub-optimal conditions?
<--- Score

101. How will the day-to-day responsibilities for monitoring and continual improvement be transferred from the improvement team to the process owner?
<--- Score

Add up total points for this section:
_____ = Total points for this section

Divided by: _____ (number of
statements answered) = _____
Average score for this section

Transfer your score to the Digital
Business Model Index at the beginning
of the Self-Assessment.

CRITERION #7: SUSTAIN:

INTENT: Retain the benefits.

In my belief, the answer to this question is clearly defined:

5 Strongly Agree

4 Agree

3 Neutral

2 Disagree

1 Strongly Disagree

1. What is the source of the strategies for Digital Business Model strengthening and reform?
<--- Score

2. Who will provide the final approval of Digital Business Model deliverables?
<--- Score

3. How do you keep the momentum going?
<--- Score

4. Who do you want your customers to become?
<--- Score

5. How do you set Digital Business Model stretch targets and how do you get people to not only participate in setting these stretch targets but also that they strive to achieve these?
<--- Score

6. If there were zero limitations, what would you do differently?
<--- Score

7. What could happen if you do not do it?
<--- Score

8. How can you negotiate Digital Business Model successfully with a stubborn boss, an irate client, or a deceitful coworker?
<--- Score

9. What is the overall business strategy?
<--- Score

10. If no one would ever find out about your accomplishments, how would you lead differently?
<--- Score

11. What are your most important goals for the strategic Digital Business Model objectives?
<--- Score

12. Which individuals, teams or departments will be involved in Digital Business Model?
<--- Score

13. How will you know that the Digital Business Model project has been successful?
<--- Score

14. Do you have the right capabilities and capacities?
<--- Score

15. Who will be responsible for deciding whether Digital Business Model goes ahead or not after the initial investigations?
<--- Score

16. Is it economical; do you have the time and money?
<--- Score

17. What information is critical to your organization that your executives are ignoring?
<--- Score

18. Are you leveraging existing capabilities and making big bets in new and innovative digital business models?
<--- Score

19. Would you rather sell to knowledgeable and informed customers or to uninformed customers?
<--- Score

20. What are the key enablers to make this Digital Business Model move?
<--- Score

21. Who will determine interim and final deadlines?
<--- Score

22. What is the purpose of Digital Business Model in

relation to the mission?
<--- Score

23. Is Digital Business Model realistic, or are you setting yourself up for failure?
<--- Score

24. When information truly is ubiquitous, when reach and connectivity are completely global, when computing resources are infinite, and when a whole new set of impossibilities are not only possible, but happening, what will that do to your business?
<--- Score

25. How will you motivate the stakeholders with the least vested interest?
<--- Score

26. Think of your Digital Business Model project, what are the main functions?
<--- Score

27. What is the range of capabilities?
<--- Score

28. How do you know if you are successful?
<--- Score

29. What business benefits will Digital Business Model goals deliver if achieved?
<--- Score

30. Are you maintaining a past–present–future perspective throughout the Digital Business Model discussion?
<--- Score

31. Who else should you help?
<--- Score

32. What are internal and external Digital Business Model relations?
<--- Score

33. Is maximizing Digital Business Model protection the same as minimizing Digital Business Model loss?
<--- Score

34. Who are four people whose careers you have enhanced?
<--- Score

35. What relationships among Digital Business Model trends do you perceive?
<--- Score

36. Is your strategy driving your strategy? Or is the way in which you allocate resources driving your strategy?
<--- Score

37. Do you have past Digital Business Model successes?
<--- Score

38. Why should people listen to you?
<--- Score

39. How do you transition from the baseline to the target?
<--- Score

40. What are specific Digital Business Model rules to follow?

<--- Score

41. What counts that you are not counting?

<--- Score

42. Who is the main stakeholder, with ultimate responsibility for driving Digital Business Model forward?

<--- Score

43. How much contingency will be available in the budget?

<--- Score

44. In the past year, what have you done (or could you have done) to increase the accurate perception of your company/brand as ethical and honest?

<--- Score

45. What trophy do you want on your mantle?

<--- Score

46. How do you ensure that implementations of Digital Business Model products are done in a way that ensures safety?

<--- Score

47. Do you say no to customers for no reason?

<--- Score

48. Why will customers want to buy your organizations products/services?

<--- Score

49. Will there be any necessary staff changes (redundancies or new hires)?
<--- Score

50. What trouble can you get into?
<--- Score

51. What you are going to do to affect the numbers?
<--- Score

52. What happens if you do not have enough funding?
<--- Score

53. What goals did you miss?
<--- Score

54. What would have to be true for the option on the table to be the best possible choice?
<--- Score

55. What is the funding source for this project?
<--- Score

56. Do you think you know, or do you know you know ?
<--- Score

57. How are you doing compared to your industry?
<--- Score

58. How do you proactively clarify deliverables and Digital Business Model quality expectations?
<--- Score

59. How do you lead with Digital Business Model in

mind?
<--- Score

60. If you had to leave your organization for a year and the only communication you could have with employees/colleagues was a single paragraph, what would you write?
<--- Score

61. How do senior leaders deploy your organizations vision and values through your leadership system, to the workforce, to key suppliers and partners, and to customers and other stakeholders, as appropriate?
<--- Score

62. Is there any reason to believe the opposite of my current belief?
<--- Score

63. How do you determine the key elements that affect Digital Business Model workforce satisfaction, how are these elements determined for different workforce groups and segments?
<--- Score

64. What is an unauthorized commitment?
<--- Score

65. Who do you think the world wants your organization to be?
<--- Score

66. What Digital Business Model modifications can you make work for you?
<--- Score

67. Are all key stakeholders present at all Structured Walkthroughs?
<--- Score

68. What role does communication play in the success or failure of a Digital Business Model project?
<--- Score

69. What are the barriers to increased Digital Business Model production?
<--- Score

70. Do you feel that more should be done in the Digital Business Model area?
<--- Score

71. Why is it important to have senior management support for a Digital Business Model project?
<--- Score

72. Marketing budgets are tighter, consumers are more skeptical, and social media has changed forever the way we talk about Digital Business Model, how do you gain traction?
<--- Score

73. Who is responsible for errors?
<--- Score

74. Is Digital Business Model dependent on the successful delivery of a current project?
<--- Score

75. Who do we want your customers to become?
<--- Score

76. How much of a contribution do you make to the shift to a digital business model?
<--- Score

77. How will you insure seamless interoperability of Digital Business Model moving forward?
<--- Score

78. Who have you, as a company, historically been when you've been at your best?
<--- Score

79. How do you govern and fulfill your societal responsibilities?
<--- Score

80. What would you recommend your friend do if he/she were facing this dilemma?
<--- Score

81. How can you become the company that would put you out of business?
<--- Score

82. Are the criteria for selecting recommendations stated?
<--- Score

83. Do you think Digital Business Model accomplishes the goals you expect it to accomplish?
<--- Score

84. How do you go about securing Digital Business Model?
<--- Score

85. Operational - will it work?
<--- Score

86. What is the estimated value of the project?
<--- Score

87. What are the challenges?
<--- Score

88. What are the long-term Digital Business Model goals?
<--- Score

89. Political -is anyone trying to undermine this project?
<--- Score

90. What Digital Business Model skills are most important?
<--- Score

91. Are the assumptions believable and achievable?
<--- Score

92. What new services of functionality will be implemented next with Digital Business Model ?
<--- Score

93. What are the top 3 things at the forefront of your Digital Business Model agendas for the next 3 years?
<--- Score

94. How do you engage the workforce, in addition to satisfying them?
<--- Score

95. What knowledge, skills and characteristics mark a good Digital Business Model project manager?
<--- Score

96. What is the kind of project structure that would be appropriate for your Digital Business Model project, should it be formal and complex, or can it be less formal and relatively simple?
<--- Score

97. How important is Digital Business Model to the user organizations mission?
<--- Score

98. What must you excel at?
<--- Score

99. Are you / should you be revolutionary or evolutionary?
<--- Score

100. Whom among your colleagues do you trust, and for what?
<--- Score

101. In a project to restructure Digital Business Model outcomes, which stakeholders would you involve?
<--- Score

102. Will it be accepted by users?
<--- Score

103. If your company went out of business tomorrow, would anyone who doesn't get a paycheck here care?
<--- Score

104. What is effective Digital Business Model?
<--- Score

105. What stupid rule would you most like to kill?
<--- Score

106. Who is responsible for ensuring appropriate resources (time, people and money) are allocated to Digital Business Model?
<--- Score

107. If you got fired and a new hire took your place, what would she do different?
<--- Score

108. What are you trying to prove to yourself, and how might it be hijacking your life and business success?
<--- Score

109. What is the overall talent health of your organization as a whole at senior levels, and for each organization reporting to a member of the Senior Leadership Team?
<--- Score

110. What have been your experiences in defining long range Digital Business Model goals?
<--- Score

111. What one word do you want to own in the minds of your customers, employees, and partners?
<--- Score

112. Where can you break convention?
<--- Score

113. Why not do Digital Business Model?
<--- Score

114. How can you become more high-tech but still be high touch?
<--- Score

115. Can you do all this work?
<--- Score

116. Are assumptions made in Digital Business Model stated explicitly?
<--- Score

117. What are your personal philosophies regarding Digital Business Model and how do they influence your work?
<--- Score

118. What are the gaps in your knowledge and experience?
<--- Score

119. If your customer were your grandmother, would you tell her to buy what you're selling?
<--- Score

120. Who uses your product in ways you never expected?
<--- Score

121. Is the Digital Business Model organization completing tasks effectively and efficiently?
<--- Score

122. How do you track customer value, profitability

or financial return, organizational success, and sustainability?
<--- Score

123. Is there any existing Digital Business Model governance structure?
<--- Score

124. If you weren't already in this business, would you enter it today? And if not, what are you going to do about it?
<--- Score

125. What is something you believe that nearly no one agrees with you on?
<--- Score

126. How long will it take to change?
<--- Score

127. What projects are going on in the organization today, and what resources are those projects using from the resource pools?
<--- Score

128. Who is responsible for Digital Business Model?
<--- Score

129. What are you challenging?
<--- Score

130. How do cryptocurrency companies create and capture value through digital business models?
<--- Score

131. Who, on the executive team or the board, has

spoken to a customer recently?

<--- Score

132. What are the short and long-term Digital Business Model goals?

<--- Score

133. Whose voice (department, ethnic group, women, older workers, etc) might you have missed hearing from in your company, and how might you amplify this voice to create positive momentum for your business?

<--- Score

134. What is your competitive advantage?

<--- Score

135. If you do not follow, then how to lead?

<--- Score

136. What is the craziest thing you can do?

<--- Score

137. Is there a work around that you can use?

<--- Score

138. How do you foster innovation?

<--- Score

139. What management system can you use to leverage the Digital Business Model experience, ideas, and concerns of the people closest to the work to be done?

<--- Score

140. How do you manage Digital Business Model

Knowledge Management (KM)?
<--- Score

141. What are the success criteria that will indicate that Digital Business Model objectives have been met and the benefits delivered?
<--- Score

142. What unique value proposition (UVP) do you offer?
<--- Score

143. Which functions and people interact with the supplier and or customer?
<--- Score

144. What are the rules and assumptions your industry operates under? What if the opposite were true?
<--- Score

145. How do you stay inspired?
<--- Score

146. What are the business goals Digital Business Model is aiming to achieve?
<--- Score

147. What potential megatrends could make your business model obsolete?
<--- Score

148. Which models, tools and techniques are necessary?
<--- Score

149. Instead of going to current contacts for new

ideas, what if you reconnected with dormant contacts--the people you used to know? If you were going reactivate a dormant tie, who would it be?
<--- Score

150. What are current Digital Business Model paradigms?
<--- Score

151. What are the essentials of internal Digital Business Model management?
<--- Score

152. How will you ensure you get what you expected?
<--- Score

153. Ask yourself: how would you do this work if you only had one staff member to do it?
<--- Score

154. Can you maintain your growth without detracting from the factors that have contributed to your success?
<--- Score

155. What should you stop doing?
<--- Score

156. What are the potential basics of Digital Business Model fraud?
<--- Score

157. What happens at your organization when people fail?
<--- Score

158. What was the last experiment you ran?
<--- Score

159. How do customers see your organization?
<--- Score

160. Which Digital Business Model goals are the most important?
<--- Score

161. Who are your customers?
<--- Score

162. How do you foster the skills, knowledge, talents, attributes, and characteristics you want to have?
<--- Score

163. How do you maintain Digital Business Model's Integrity?
<--- Score

164. How can you incorporate support to ensure safe and effective use of Digital Business Model into the services that you provide?
<--- Score

165. What will be the consequences to the stakeholder (financial, reputation etc) if Digital Business Model does not go ahead or fails to deliver the objectives?
<--- Score

166. Can the schedule be done in the given time?
<--- Score

167. How do you provide a safe environment

-physically and emotionally?
<--- Score

168. What does your signature ensure?
<--- Score

169. What is your Digital Business Model strategy?
<--- Score

170. If you had to rebuild your organization without any traditional competitive advantages (i.e., no killer technology, promising research, innovative product/ service delivery model, etcetera), how would your people have to approach their work and collaborate together in order to create the necessary conditions for success?
<--- Score

171. If you find that you havent accomplished one of the goals for one of the steps of the Digital Business Model strategy, what will you do to fix it?
<--- Score

172. If you were responsible for initiating and implementing major changes in your organization, what steps might you take to ensure acceptance of those changes?
<--- Score

173. What have you done to protect your business from competitive encroachment?
<--- Score

174. Is your basic point _____ or _____?
<--- Score

175. What is your BATNA (best alternative to a negotiated agreement)?
<--- Score

176. How do you make it meaningful in connecting Digital Business Model with what users do day-to-day?
<--- Score

177. What is your formula for success in Digital Business Model ?
<--- Score

178. Why is Digital Business Model important for you now?
<--- Score

179. How likely is it that a customer would recommend your company to a friend or colleague?
<--- Score

180. How do you accomplish your long range Digital Business Model goals?
<--- Score

181. In retrospect, of the projects that you pulled the plug on, what percent do you wish had been allowed to keep going, and what percent do you wish had ended earlier?
<--- Score

182. What is your question? Why?
<--- Score

183. To whom do you add value?
<--- Score

184. Who are the key stakeholders?
<--- Score

Add up total points for this section:
_ _ _ _ _ = Total points for this section

Divided by: _ _ _ _ _ _ (number of
statements answered) = _ _ _ _ _ _
Average score for this section

Transfer your score to the Digital
Business Model Index at the beginning
of the Self-Assessment.

Digital Business Model and Managing Projects, Criteria for Project Managers:

1.0 Initiating Process Group: Digital Business Model

1. What do you need to do?

2. What input will you be required to provide the Digital Business Model project team?

3. How will you know you did it?

4. Who is funding the Digital Business Model project?

5. When must it be done?

6. When will the Digital Business Model project be done?

7. How well did the chosen processes fit the needs of the Digital Business Model project?

8. Were escalated issues resolved promptly?

9. What will you do?

10. Who supports, improves, and oversees standardized processes related to the Digital Business Model projects program?

11. Who is behind the Digital Business Model project?

12. Realistic - are the desired results expressed in a way that the team will be motivated and believe that the required level of involvement will be obtained?

13. During which stage of Risk planning are modeling

techniques used to determine overall effects of risks on Digital Business Model project objectives for high probability, high impact risks?

14. How well did the chosen processes produce the expected results?

15. How can you make your needs known?

16. How will it affect me?

17. Did the Digital Business Model project team have the right skills?

18. Who does what?

19. What is the stake of others in your Digital Business Model project?

20. When are the deliverables to be generated in each phase?

1.1 Project Charter: Digital Business Model

21. Why use a Digital Business Model project charter?

22. What are the deliverables?

23. What are some examples of a business case?

24. Who are the stakeholders?

25. Major high-level milestone targets: what events measure progress?

26. Assumptions and constraints: what assumptions were made in defining the Digital Business Model project?

27. If finished, on what date did it finish?

28. What is the justification?

29. What changes can you make to improve?

30. Name and describe the elements that deal with providing the detail?

31. What is the business need?

32. Why have you chosen the aim you have set forth?

33. What date will the task finish?

34. What goes into your Digital Business Model project Charter?

35. What are you trying to accomplish?

36. Where does all this information come from?

37. How will you learn more about the process or system you are trying to improve?

38. What outcome, in measureable terms, are you hoping to accomplish?

39. Market – identify products market, including whether it is outside of the objective: what is the purpose of the program or Digital Business Model project?

1.2 Stakeholder Register: Digital Business Model

40. What is the power of the stakeholder?

41. What & Why?

42. Is your organization ready for change?

43. How should employers make voices heard?

44. What are the major Digital Business Model project milestones requiring communications or providing communications opportunities?

45. Who wants to talk about Security?

46. How much influence do they have on the Digital Business Model project?

47. How will reports be created?

48. How big is the gap?

49. What opportunities exist to provide communications?

50. Who is managing stakeholder engagement?

1.3 Stakeholder Analysis Matrix: Digital Business Model

51. What is the relationship among stakeholders?

52. Is changing technology threatening your organizations position?

53. Market demand?

54. Legislative effects?

55. Global influences?

56. Are there people who ise voices or interests in the issue may not be heard?

57. Who determines value?

58. Is there evidence that demonstrates the impact of education on the Digital Business Model projects outcomes?

59. Niche target markets?

60. Political effects?

61. How to measure the achievement of the Development Objective?

62. Geographical, export, import?

63. Competitor intentions - various?

64. Technology development and innovation?

65. Who has control over whom?

66. Vital contracts and partners?

67. It developments?

68. What advantages do your organizations stakeholders have?

69. What is your organizations competitors doing?

70. Do any safeguard policies apply to the Digital Business Model project?

2.0 Planning Process Group: Digital Business Model

71. If a risk event occurs, what will you do?

72. How well do the team follow the chosen processes?

73. Are the follow-up indicators relevant and do they meet the quality needed to measure the outputs and outcomes of the Digital Business Model project?

74. You did your readings, yes?

75. What types of differentiated effects are resulting from the Digital Business Model project and to what extent?

76. The Digital Business Model project charter is created in which Digital Business Model project management process group?

77. Why do it Digital Business Model projects fail?

78. If task x starts two days late, what is the effect on the Digital Business Model project end date?

79. Explanation: is what the Digital Business Model project intents to solve a hard question?

80. Are there efficient coordination mechanisms to avoid overloading the counterparts, participating stakeholders?

81. If you are late, will anybody notice?

82. What is the difference between the early schedule and late schedule?

83. How well will the chosen processes produce the expected results?

84. To what extent is the program helping to influence your organizations policy framework?

85. Who are the Digital Business Model project stakeholders?

86. Are you just doing busywork to pass the time?

87. In what way has the program contributed towards the issue culture and development included on the public agenda?

88. What type of estimation method are you using?

89. To what extent and in what ways are the Digital Business Model project contributing to progress towards organizational reform?

90. What will you do to minimize the impact should a risk event occur?

2.1 Project Management Plan: Digital Business Model

91. Why do you manage integration?

92. Are calculations and results of analyzes essentially correct?

93. Are there non-structural buyout or relocation recommendations?

94. Are cost risk analysis methods applied to develop contingencies for the estimated total Digital Business Model project costs?

95. What are the assigned resources?

96. What worked well?

97. How do you organize the costs in the Digital Business Model project management plan?

98. Are there any scope changes proposed for a previously authorized Digital Business Model project?

99. How do you manage integration?

100. Does the selected plan protect privacy?

101. How can you best help your organization to develop consistent practices in Digital Business Model project management planning stages?

102. What went wrong?

103. Is there anything you would now do differently on your Digital Business Model project based on past experience?

104. Are the proposed Digital Business Model project purposes different than a previously authorized Digital Business Model project?

105. What is risk management?

106. Who is the Digital Business Model project Manager?

107. Is the budget realistic?

108. How do you manage time?

109. Is mitigation authorized or recommended?

2.2 Scope Management Plan: Digital Business Model

110. Has the budget been baselined?

111. Which statement about customer expectations is not true?

112. Do all stakeholders know how to access this repository and where to find the Digital Business Model project documentation?

113. Without-plan conditions?

114. Are you doing what you have set out to do?

115. Are you meeting with stake holders and team members?

116. Have all documents been archived in a Digital Business Model project repository for each release?

117. Were Digital Business Model project team members involved in detailed estimating and scheduling?

118. Are the proposed Digital Business Model project purposes different than the previously authorized Digital Business Model project?

119. Has your organization done similar tasks before?

120. Who is doing what for whom?

121. Is current scope of the Digital Business Model project substantially different than that originally defined?

122. What is the need the Digital Business Model project will address?

123. Are enough systems & user personnel assigned to the Digital Business Model project?

124. Does the title convey to the reader the essence of the Digital Business Model project?

125. Are Digital Business Model project team members involved in detailed estimating and scheduling?

126. Are all payments made according to the contract(s)?

127. During what part of the PM process is the Digital Business Model project scope statement created?

128. Is there a set of procedures defining the scope, procedures, and deliverables defining quality control?

129. What are the Quality Assurance overheads?

2.3 Requirements Management Plan: Digital Business Model

130. How will unresolved questions be handled once approval has been obtained?

131. Who has the authority to reject Digital Business Model project requirements?

132. Who will do the reporting and to whom will reports be delivered?

133. Have stakeholders been instructed in the Change Control process?

134. Does the Digital Business Model project have a Change Control process?

135. Do you understand the role that each stakeholder will play in the requirements process?

136. Did you distinguish the scope of work the contractor(s) will be required to do?

137. Will you perform a Requirements Risk assessment and develop a plan to deal with risks?

138. Are actual resources expenditures versus planned expenditures acceptable?

139. How detailed should the Digital Business Model project get?

140. Controlling Digital Business Model project requirements involves monitoring the status of the Digital Business Model project requirements and managing changes to the requirements. Who is responsible for monitoring and tracking the Digital Business Model project requirements?

141. Is it new or replacing an existing business system or process?

142. Business analysis scope?

143. Who will approve the requirements (and if multiple approvers, in what order)?

144. Did you avoid subjective, flowery or non-specific statements?

145. Should you include sub-activities?

146. How will the information be distributed?

147. Is there formal agreement on who has authority to approve a change in requirements?

148. Are actual resource expenditures versus planned still acceptable?

149. How will the requirements become prioritized?

2.4 Requirements Documentation: Digital Business Model

150. How linear / iterative is your Requirements Gathering process (or will it be)?

151. The problem with gathering requirements is right there in the word gathering. What images does it conjure?

152. Is the requirement realistically testable?

153. How do you know when a Requirement is accurate enough?

154. Where are business rules being captured?

155. If applicable; are there issues linked with the fact that this is an offshore Digital Business Model project?

156. What is the risk associated with cost and schedule?

157. Who provides requirements?

158. Are there legal issues?

159. What are current process problems?

160. Who is interacting with the system?

161. Does the system provide the functions which best support the customers needs?

162. Does your organization restrict technical alternatives?

163. How does what is being described meet the business need?

164. What can tools do for us?

165. What is effective documentation?

166. Is new technology needed?

167. Who is involved?

168. What is a show stopper in the requirements?

169. Are all functions required by the customer included?

2.5 Requirements Traceability Matrix: Digital Business Model

170. Why use a WBS?

171. What is the WBS?

172. Is there a requirements traceability process in place?

173. How will it affect the stakeholders personally in career?

174. How do you manage scope?

175. How small is small enough?

176. Will you use a Requirements Traceability Matrix?

177. Why do you manage scope?

178. What are the chronologies, contingencies, consequences, criteria?

179. Do you have a clear understanding of all subcontracts in place?

180. Describe the process for approving requirements so they can be added to the traceability matrix and Digital Business Model project work can be performed. Will the Digital Business Model project requirements become approved in writing?

181. What percentage of Digital Business Model projects are producing traceability matrices between requirements and other work products?

2.6 Project Scope Statement: Digital Business Model

182. Will the risk plan be updated on a regular and frequent basis?

183. Were potential customers involved early in the planning process?

184. Elements that deal with providing the detail?

185. Will this process be communicated to the customer and Digital Business Model project team?

186. Is the plan for your organization of the Digital Business Model project resources adequate?

187. Elements of scope management that deal with concept development ?

188. If the scope changes, what will the impact be to your Digital Business Model project in terms of duration, cost, quality, or any other important areas of the Digital Business Model project?

189. What are the defined meeting materials?

190. If there are vendors, have they signed off on the Digital Business Model project Plan?

191. How will you verify the accuracy of the work of the Digital Business Model project, and what constitutes acceptance of the deliverables?

192. Why do you need to manage scope?

193. Will the qa related information be reported regularly as part of the status reporting mechanisms?

194. Is the change control process documented and on file?

195. Is there a baseline plan against which to measure progress?

196. Is the scope of your Digital Business Model project well defined?

197. Once its defined, what is the stability of the Digital Business Model project scope?

198. Are there backup strategies for key members of the Digital Business Model project?

199. Will an issue form be in use?

200. Will the risk status be reported to management on a regular and frequent basis?

2.7 Assumption and Constraint Log: Digital Business Model

201. What other teams / processes would be impacted by changes to the current process, and how?

202. What is positive about the current process?

203. What if failure during recovery?

204. Are there ways to reduce the time it takes to get something approved?

205. Does the plan conform to standards?

206. Have Digital Business Model project management standards and procedures been established and documented?

207. If appropriate, is the deliverable content consistent with current Digital Business Model project documents and in compliance with the Document Management Plan?

208. Have adequate resources been provided by management to ensure Digital Business Model project success?

209. Are there processes in place to ensure that all the terms and code concepts have been documented consistently?

210. What does an audit system look like?

211. Are processes for release management of new development from coding and unit testing, to integration testing, to training, and production defined and followed?

212. Does the document/deliverable meet all requirements (for example, statement of work) specific to this deliverable?

213. Violation trace: why ?

214. What threats might prevent you from getting there?

215. Are there nonconformance issues?

216. What do you log?

217. Have you eliminated all duplicative tasks or manual efforts, where appropriate?

218. Has a Digital Business Model project Communications Plan been developed?

219. Is the process working, and people are not executing in compliance of the process?

2.8 Work Breakdown Structure: Digital Business Model

220. How big is a work-package?

221. What is the probability that the Digital Business Model project duration will exceed xx weeks?

222. When do you stop?

223. Is it still viable?

224. Who has to do it?

225. How will you and your Digital Business Model project team define the Digital Business Model projects scope and work breakdown structure?

226. How many levels?

227. How far down?

228. When does it have to be done?

229. Is it a change in scope?

230. Where does it take place?

231. How much detail?

232. When would you develop a Work Breakdown Structure?

233. Do you need another level?

234. What is the probability of completing the Digital Business Model project in less that xx days?

235. Why is it useful?

236. Why would you develop a Work Breakdown Structure?

2.9 WBS Dictionary: Digital Business Model

237. Are records maintained to show how management reserves are used?

238. Time-phased control account budgets?

239. Are work packages assigned to performing organizations?

240. Are current budgets resulting from changes to the authorized work and/or internal replanning, reconcilable to original budgets for specified reporting items?

241. Identify and isolate causes of favorable and unfavorable cost and schedule variances?

242. Detailed schedules which support control account and work package start and completion dates/events?

243. Does the accounting system provide a basis for auditing records of direct costs chargeable to the contract?

244. Can the contractor substantiate work package and planning package budgets?

245. Does the contractors system identify work accomplishment against the schedule plan?

246. Are estimates developed by Digital Business Model project personnel coordinated with the already stated responsible for overall management to determine whether required resources will be available according to revised planning?

247. The anticipated business volume?

248. Where engineering standards or other internal work measurement systems are used, is there a formal relationship between corresponding values and work package budgets?

249. Appropriate work authorization documents which subdivide the contractual effort and responsibilities, within functional organizations?

250. Is cost performance measurement at the point in time most suitable for the category of material involved, and no earlier than the time of actual receipt of material?

251. Are estimates of costs at completion generated in a rational, consistent manner?

252. Are the bases and rates for allocating costs from each indirect pool to commercial work consistent with the already stated used to allocate corresponding costs to Government contracts?

253. Are your organizations and items of cost assigned to each pool identified?

254. Are records maintained to show how undistributed budgets are controlled?

255. Are control accounts opened and closed based on the start and completion of work contained therein?

256. Does the sum of all work package budgets plus planning packages within control accounts equal the budgets assigned to the already stated control accounts?

2.10 Schedule Management Plan: Digital Business Model

257. Are the processes for status updates and maintenance defined?

258. Is a process for scheduling and reporting defined, including forms and formats?

259. Timeline and milestones?

260. Is your organization certified as a supplier, wholesaler and/or regular dealer?

261. Quality assurance overheads?

262. Is the communication plan being followed?

263. Are corrective actions and variances reported?

264. What weaknesses do you have?

265. Does the Digital Business Model project have a formal Digital Business Model project Charter?

266. Does the schedule have reasonable float?

267. Have Digital Business Model project management standards and procedures been identified / established and documented?

268. Is there an onboarding process in place?

269. Is the ims development and management approach described?

270. Alignment to strategic goals & objectives?

271. Does the ims reflect accurate current status and credible start/finish forecasts for all to-go tasks and milestones?

272. Are the schedule estimates reasonable given the Digital Business Model project?

273. Are all vendor contracts closed out?

274. Does the Digital Business Model project have a Statement of Work?

275. Have Digital Business Model project team accountabilities & responsibilities been clearly defined?

276. Staffing Requirements?

2.11 Activity List: Digital Business Model

277. What will be performed?

278. Where will it be performed?

279. Is there anything planned that does not need to be here?

280. Is infrastructure setup part of your Digital Business Model project?

281. What is the total time required to complete the Digital Business Model project if no delays occur?

282. What are the critical bottleneck activities?

283. How do you determine the late start (LS) for each activity?

284. For other activities, how much delay can be tolerated?

285. What is the LF and LS for each activity?

286. When do the individual activities need to start and finish?

287. What went well?

288. How much slack is available in the Digital Business Model project?

289. How should ongoing costs be monitored to try to keep the Digital Business Model project within budget?

290. Who will perform the work?

291. What are you counting on?

292. How can the Digital Business Model project be displayed graphically to better visualize the activities?

293. Are the required resources available or need to be acquired?

294. How difficult will it be to do specific activities on this Digital Business Model project?

295. When will the work be performed?

2.12 Activity Attributes: Digital Business Model

296. Where else does it apply?

297. Are the required resources available?

298. What is missing?

299. What conclusions/generalizations can you draw from this?

300. Has management defined a definite timeframe for the turnaround or Digital Business Model project window?

301. How much activity detail is required?

302. Can more resources be added?

303. Were there other ways you could have organized the data to achieve similar results?

304. How else could the items be grouped?

305. What is the general pattern here?

306. How difficult will it be to complete specific activities on this Digital Business Model project?

307. Have constraints been applied to the start and finish milestones for the phases?

308. What went right?

309. How difficult will it be to do specific activities on this Digital Business Model project?

310. Resource is assigned to?

311. Activity: what is Missing?

312. What is your organizations history in doing similar activities?

2.13 Milestone List: Digital Business Model

313. When will the Digital Business Model project be complete?

314. What specific improvements did you make to the Digital Business Model project proposal since the previous time?

315. New USPs?

316. Which path is the critical path?

317. Describe the concept of the technology, product or service that will be or has been developed. How will it be used?

318. Insurmountable weaknesses?

319. How late can each activity be finished and started?

320. How will the milestone be verified?

321. Information and research?

322. Reliability of data, plan predictability?

323. Environmental effects?

324. What background experience, skills, and strengths does the team bring to your organization?

325. How difficult will it be to do specific activities on this Digital Business Model project?

326. How soon can the activity start?

327. Timescales, deadlines and pressures?

328. Describe your organizations strengths and core competencies. What factors will make your organization succeed?

329. Describe the industry you are in and the market growth opportunities. What is the market for your technology, product or service?

2.14 Network Diagram: Digital Business Model

330. Where do you schedule uncertainty time?

331. How difficult will it be to do specific activities on this Digital Business Model project?

332. Can you calculate the confidence level?

333. What is the probability of completing the Digital Business Model project in less that xx days?

334. What activities must follow this activity?

335. What are the Key Success Factors?

336. Are the gantt chart and/or network diagram updated periodically and used to assess the overall Digital Business Model project timetable?

337. Review the logical flow of the network diagram. Take a look at which activities you have first and then sequence the activities. Do they make sense?

338. What controls the start and finish of a job?

339. What must be completed before an activity can be started?

340. What is the completion time?

341. Where do schedules come from?

342. How confident can you be in your milestone dates and the delivery date?

343. Why must you schedule milestones, such as reviews, throughout the Digital Business Model project?

344. What job or jobs could run concurrently?

345. What job or jobs follow it?

346. Which type of network diagram allows you to depict four types of dependencies?

347. If the Digital Business Model project network diagram cannot change and you have extra personnel resources, what is the BEST thing to do?

2.15 Activity Resource Requirements: Digital Business Model

348. Time for overtime?

349. Organizational Applicability?

350. Which logical relationship does the PDM use most often?

351. How many signatures do you require on a check and does this match what is in your policy and procedures?

352. Anything else?

353. When does monitoring begin?

354. Why do you do that?

355. Do you use tools like decomposition and rolling-wave planning to produce the activity list and other outputs?

356. What are constraints that you might find during the Human Resource Planning process?

357. Other support in specific areas?

358. What is the Work Plan Standard?

359. How do you handle petty cash?

360. Are there unresolved issues that need to be addressed?

2.16 Resource Breakdown Structure: Digital Business Model

361. Who is allowed to perform which functions?

362. Goals for the Digital Business Model project. What is each stakeholders desired outcome for the Digital Business Model project?

363. Any changes from stakeholders?

364. The list could probably go on, but, the thing that you would most like to know is, How long & How much?

365. How should the information be delivered?

366. Who delivers the information?

367. Why do you do it?

368. What is the purpose of assigning and documenting responsibility?

369. How can this help you with team building?

370. Is predictive resource analysis being done?

371. Which resources should be in the resource pool?

372. What is Digital Business Model project communication management?

373. Who will be used as a Digital Business Model project team member?

374. When do they need the information?

375. What is the primary purpose of the human resource plan?

376. What are the requirements for resource data?

2.17 Activity Duration Estimates: Digital Business Model

377. Is a formal written notice that the contract is complete provided to the seller?

378. Can they use the already stated?

379. Does a process exist to identify Digital Business Model project roles, responsibilities and reporting relationships?

380. Based on , if you need to shorten the duration of the Digital Business Model project, what activity would you try to shorten?

381. Is a contract change control system defined to manage changes to contract terms and conditions?

382. Consider the common sources of risk on information technology Digital Business Model projects and suggestions for managing them. Which suggestions do you find most useful?

383. Are procurement documents used to solicit accurate and complete proposals from prospective sellers?

384. Which includes asking team members about the time estimates for activities and reaching agreement on the calendar date for each activity?

385. Are inspections completed to determine if the

results comply with the requirements?

386. Why is there a growing trend in outsourcing, especially in the government?

387. Are steps identified by which Digital Business Model project documents may be changed?

388. Does a process exist for approving or rejecting changes?

389. Does a process exist to identify which qualified resources may be attainable?

390. Are risks monitored to determine if an event has occurred or if the mitigation was successful?

391. What is the duration of a milestone?

392. Do you think Digital Business Model project managers of large information technology Digital Business Model projects need strong technical skills?

393. Which frame seemed to be the most important and why?

394. Is a contract developed which obligates the seller and the buyer?

395. What functions does this software provide that cannot be done easily using other tools such as a spreadsheet or database?

2.18 Duration Estimating Worksheet: Digital Business Model

396. Can the Digital Business Model project be constructed as planned?

397. Science = process: remember the scientific method?

398. Will the Digital Business Model project collaborate with the local community and leverage resources?

399. Done before proceeding with this activity or what can be done concurrently?

400. How should ongoing costs be monitored to try to keep the Digital Business Model project within budget?

401. Small or large Digital Business Model project?

402. What is your role?

403. Why estimate time and cost?

404. Why estimate costs?

405. What is the total time required to complete the Digital Business Model project if no delays occur?

406. Is the Digital Business Model project responsive to community need?

407. How can the Digital Business Model project be displayed graphically to better visualize the activities?

408. Is a construction detail attached (to aid in explanation)?

409. What questions do you have?

410. Value pocket identification & quantification what are value pockets?

411. What utility impacts are there?

412. What is cost and Digital Business Model project cost management?

413. Does the Digital Business Model project provide innovative ways for stakeholders to overcome obstacles or deliver better outcomes?

2.19 Project Schedule: Digital Business Model

414. Did the Digital Business Model project come in on schedule?

415. Why or why not?

416. Why is this particularly bad?

417. What is the most mis-scheduled part of process?

418. Why do you think schedule issues often cause the most conflicts on Digital Business Model projects?

419. What is Digital Business Model project management?

420. Is the Digital Business Model project schedule available for all Digital Business Model project team members to review?

421. Should you have a test for each code module?

422. What does that mean?

423. Verify that the update is accurate. Are all remaining durations correct?

424. If you can not fix it, how do you do it differently?

425. How do you manage Digital Business Model project Risk?

426. How can you fix it?

427. Was the Digital Business Model project schedule reviewed by all stakeholders and formally accepted?

428. What is risk?

429. Are there activities that came from a template or previous Digital Business Model project that are not applicable on this phase of this Digital Business Model project?

430. Why time management?

431. How can you shorten the schedule?

2.20 Cost Management Plan: Digital Business Model

432. Are vendor contract reports, reviews and visits conducted periodically?

433. Planning and scheduling responsibilities – How will the responsibilities for planning and scheduling be allocated?

434. Is quality monitored from the perspective of the customers needs and expectations?

435. Is the Digital Business Model project schedule available for all Digital Business Model project team members to review?

436. Progress measurement and control – How will the Digital Business Model project measure and control progress?

437. Is a pmo (Digital Business Model project management office) in place and provide oversight to the Digital Business Model project?

438. Is current scope of the Digital Business Model project substantially different than that originally defined?

439. Does the schedule include Digital Business Model project management time and change request analysis time?

440. Have key stakeholders been identified?

441. Are the key elements of a Digital Business Model project Charter present?

442. Is it possible to track all classes of Digital Business Model project work (e.g. scheduled, un-scheduled, defect repair, etc.)?

443. Are vendor invoices audited for accuracy before payment?

444. Are the Digital Business Model project team members located locally to the users/stakeholders?

445. Are written status reports provided on a designated frequent basis?

446. Have all necessary approvals been obtained?

447. What does this mean to a cost or scheduler manager?

448. Have the reasons why the changes to your organizational systems and capabilities are required?

2.21 Activity Cost Estimates: Digital Business Model

449. Measurable - are the targets measurable?

450. Does the estimator have experience?

451. Who determines the quality and expertise of contractors?

452. Performance bond should always provide what part of the contract value?

453. Which contract type places the most risk on the seller?

454. How and when do you enter into Digital Business Model project Procurement Management?

455. Was it performed on time?

456. Was the consultant knowledgeable about the program?

457. Can you change your activities?

458. Estimated cost?

459. What cost data should be used to estimate costs during the 2-year follow-up period?

460. Does the activity rely on a common set of tools to carry it out?

461. Will you use any tools, such as Digital Business Model project management software, to assist in capturing Earned Value metrics?

462. How Award?

463. Did the Digital Business Model project team have the right skills?

464. Eac -estimate at completion, what is the total job expected to cost?

465. How quickly can the task be done with the skills available?

466. Were the tasks or work products prepared by the consultant useful?

467. What areas were overlooked on this Digital Business Model project?

468. What is the last item a Digital Business Model project manager must do to finalize Digital Business Model project close-out?

2.22 Cost Estimating Worksheet: Digital Business Model

469. What info is needed?

470. What can be included?

471. What additional Digital Business Model project(s) could be initiated as a result of this Digital Business Model project?

472. Is the Digital Business Model project responsive to community need?

473. Does the Digital Business Model project provide innovative ways for stakeholders to overcome obstacles or deliver better outcomes?

474. Is it feasible to establish a control group arrangement?

475. What will others want?

476. How will the results be shared and to whom?

477. Identify the timeframe necessary to monitor progress and collect data to determine how the selected measure has changed?

478. What happens to any remaining funds not used?

479. Ask: are others positioned to know, are others credible, and will others cooperate?

480. What costs are to be estimated?

481. Can a trend be established from historical performance data on the selected measure and are the criteria for using trend analysis or forecasting methods met?

482. Will the Digital Business Model project collaborate with the local community and leverage resources?

483. What is the estimated labor cost today based upon this information?

484. Who is best positioned to know and assist in identifying corresponding factors?

485. What is the purpose of estimating?

2.23 Cost Baseline: Digital Business Model

486. What deliverables come first?

487. Has the documentation relating to operation and maintenance of the product(s) or service(s) been delivered to, and accepted by, operations management?

488. Is there anything you need from upper management in order to be successful?

489. How long are you willing to wait before you find out were late?

490. What does a good WBS NOT look like?

491. Definition of done can be traced back to the definitions of what are you providing to the customer in terms of deliverables?

492. Is the requested change request a result of changes in other Digital Business Model project(s)?

493. Why do you manage cost?

494. Impact to environment?

495. How accurate do cost estimates need to be?

496. On budget?

497. Who will use corresponding metrics ?

498. When should cost estimates be developed?

499. Digital Business Model project goals -should others be reconsidered?

500. On time?

501. How likely is it to go wrong?

502. What is your organizations history in doing similar tasks?

2.24 Quality Management Plan: Digital Business Model

503. Does the program use other agents to collect samples?

504. Was trending evident between audits?

505. Why quality management?

506. Is there a Quality Management Plan?

507. Do the data quality objectives communicate the intended program need?

508. Does a documented Digital Business Model project organizational policy & plan (i.e. governance model) exist?

509. How is staff trained on the recording of field notes?

510. How do your action plans support the strategic objectives?

511. Can it be done better?

512. Who is responsible for writing the qapp?

513. How are people conducting sampling trained?

514. How does your organization measure customer satisfaction/dissatisfaction?

515. You know what your customers expectations are regarding this process?

516. Checking the completeness and appropriateness of the sampling and testing. Were the right locations/samples tested for the right parameters?

517. What procedures are used to determine if you use, and the number of split, replicate or duplicate samples taken at a site?

518. Can you perform this task or activity in a more effective manner?

519. How are training records kept?

520. How does your organization decide what to measure?

521. Who needs a qmp?

522. Is this process still needed?

2.25 Quality Metrics: Digital Business Model

523. What can manufacturing professionals do to ensure quality is seen as an integral part of the entire product lifecycle?

524. What documentation is required?

525. What is the timeline to meet your goal?

526. Was review conducted per standard protocols?

527. Are interface issues coordinated?

528. Is the reporting frequency appropriate?

529. Subjective quality component: customer satisfaction, how do you measure it?

530. What metrics do you measure?

531. If the defect rate during testing is substantially higher than that of the previous release (or a similar product), then ask: Did you plan for and actually improve testing effectiveness?

532. What forces exist that would cause them to change?

533. What method of measurement do you use?

534. Which data do others need in one place to target

areas of improvement?

535. What percentage are outcome-based?

536. There are many reasons to shore up quality-related metrics, and what metrics are important?

537. Were quality attributes reported?

538. Is material complete (and does it meet the standards)?

539. Which are the right metrics to use?

540. What metrics are important and most beneficial to measure?

541. Are quality metrics defined?

2.26 Process Improvement Plan: Digital Business Model

542. Does explicit definition of the measures exist?

543. Has a process guide to collect the data been developed?

544. Who should prepare the process improvement action plan?

545. Are you making progress on the goals?

546. To elicit goal statements, do you ask a question such as, What do you want to achieve?

547. Purpose of goal: the motive is determined by asking, why do you want to achieve this goal?

548. Has the time line required to move measurement results from the points of collection to databases or users been established?

549. The motive is determined by asking, Why do you want to achieve this goal?

550. Modeling current processes is great, and will you ever see a return on that investment?

551. What actions are needed to address the problems and achieve the goals?

552. Where do you focus?

553. Management commitment at all levels?

554. What lessons have you learned so far?

555. What personnel are the champions for the initiative?

556. Why do you want to achieve the goal?

557. Are you following the quality standards?

558. Have the supporting tools been developed or acquired?

559. Where are you now?

560. What makes people good SPI coaches?

561. What personnel are the change agents for your initiative?

2.27 Responsibility Assignment Matrix: Digital Business Model

562. Will too many Communicating responsibilities tangle the Digital Business Model project in unnecessary communications?

563. Changes in the nature of the overhead requirements?

564. The staff characteristics – is the group or the person capable to work together as a team?

565. Does each role with Accountable responsibility have the authority within your organization to make the required decisions?

566. Are indirect costs charged to the appropriate indirect pools and incurring organization?

567. Does a missing responsibility indicate that the current Digital Business Model project is not yet fully understood?

568. Is budgeted cost for work performed calculated in a manner consistent with the way work is planned?

569. Is data disseminated to the contractors management timely, accurate, and usable?

570. Are data elements reconcilable between internal summary reports and reports forwarded to stakeholders?

571. Are meaningful indicators identified for use in measuring the status of cost and schedule performance?

572. Are all elements of indirect expense identified to overhead cost budgets of Digital Business Model projections?

573. Too many as: does a proper segregation of duties exist?

574. The already stated responsible for overhead performance control of related costs?

575. Does each activity-deliverable have exactly one Accountable responsibility, so that accountability is clear and decisions can be made quickly?

576. Are the requirements for all items of overhead established by rational, traceable processes?

577. Direct labor dollars and/or hours?

578. What are the constraints?

579. Identify potential or actual budget-based and time-based schedule variances?

2.28 Roles and Responsibilities: Digital Business Model

580. Is the data complete?

581. What is working well?

582. Implementation of actions: Who are the responsible units?

583. Was the expectation clearly communicated?

584. Are your budgets supportive of a culture of quality data?

585. Do the values and practices inherent in the culture of your organization foster or hinder the process?

586. What specific behaviors did you observe?

587. Is feedback clearly communicated and non-judgmental?

588. What should you do now to prepare for your career 5+ years from now?

589. Are Digital Business Model project team roles and responsibilities identified and documented?

590. Who: who is involved?

591. Are governance roles and responsibilities

documented?

592. Once the responsibilities are defined for the Digital Business Model project, have the deliverables, roles and responsibilities been clearly communicated to every participant?

593. What expectations were NOT met?

594. Be specific; avoid generalities. Thank you and great work alone are insufficient. What exactly do you appreciate and why?

595. What should you highlight for improvement?

596. To decide whether to use a quality measurement, ask how will you know when it is achieved?

597. Does your vision/mission support a culture of quality data?

2.29 Human Resource Management Plan: Digital Business Model

598. Is there any form of automated support for Issues Management?

599. Has a capability assessment been conducted?

600. Is documentation created for communication with the suppliers and Vendors?

601. Does a documented Digital Business Model project organizational policy & plan (i.e. governance model) exist?

602. Personnel with expertise?

603. Does the Digital Business Model project have a formal Digital Business Model project Charter?

604. Do you have the reasons why the changes to your organizational systems and capabilities are required?

605. Has a sponsor been identified?

606. Were the budget estimates reasonable?

607. Have lessons learned been conducted after each Digital Business Model project release?

608. Are target dates established for each milestone deliverable?

609. What were things that you need to improve?

610. Digital Business Model project definition & scope?

611. How does the proposed individual meet each requirement?

612. Are adequate resources provided for the quality assurance function?

613. Were Digital Business Model project team members involved in detailed estimating and scheduling?

614. Is the quality assurance team identified?

615. What is this Digital Business Model project aiming to achieve?

2.30 Communications Management Plan: Digital Business Model

616. Is the stakeholder role recognized by your organization?

617. Where do team members get information?

618. Who is responsible?

619. What to learn?

620. Will messages be directly related to the release strategy or phases of the Digital Business Model project?

621. Are there common objectives between the team and the stakeholder?

622. How were corresponding initiatives successful?

623. Conflict resolution -which method when?

624. Who have you worked with in past, similar initiatives?

625. What does the stakeholder need from the team?

626. Who to share with?

627. How is this initiative related to other portfolios, programs, or Digital Business Model projects?

628. How often do you engage with stakeholders?

629. What steps can you take for a positive relationship?

630. Why is stakeholder engagement important?

631. What is Digital Business Model project communications management?

632. What is the political influence?

633. What are the interrelationships?

634. Who are the members of the governing body?

2.31 Risk Management Plan: Digital Business Model

635. Do end-users have realistic expectations?

636. Are people attending meetings and doing work?

637. How is the audit profession changing?

638. Maximize short-term return on investment?

639. Does the customer have a solid idea of what is required?

640. Are you on schedule?

641. Why might it be late?

642. Are flexibility and reuse paramount?

643. Is there anything you would now do differently on your Digital Business Model project based on this experience?

644. How much risk can you tolerate?

645. How can the process be made more effective or less cumbersome (process improvements)?

646. Is the customer technically sophisticated in the product area?

647. Is Digital Business Model project scope stable?

648. How will the Digital Business Model project know if your organizations risk response actions were effective?

649. Can the risk be avoided by choosing a different alternative?

650. How do you manage Digital Business Model project Risk?

651. Have staff received necessary training?

652. My Digital Business Model project leader has suddenly left your organization, what do you do?

653. Why is product liability a serious issue?

2.32 Risk Register: Digital Business Model

654. How could corresponding Risk affect the Digital Business Model project in terms of cost and schedule?

655. What evidence do you have to justify the likelihood score of the risk (audit, incident report, claim, complaints, inspection, internal review)?

656. How often will the Risk Management Plan and Risk Register be formally reviewed, and by whom?

657. Contingency actions - planned actions to reduce the immediate seriousness of the risk when it does occur. What should you do when?

658. Manageability – have mitigations to the risk been identified?

659. User involvement: do you have the right users?

660. Methodology: how will risk management be performed on this Digital Business Model project?

661. What should the audit role be in establishing a risk management process?

662. What would the impact to the Digital Business Model project objectives be should the risk arise?

663. Have other controls and solutions been implemented in other services which could be

applied as an alternative to additional funding?

664. When is it going to be done?

665. Are your objectives at risk?

666. Budget and schedule: what are the estimated costs and schedules for performing risk-related activities?

667. Having taken action, how did the responses effect change, and where is the Digital Business Model project now?

668. How well are risks controlled?

669. Market risk -will the new service or product be useful to your organization or marketable to others?

670. What may happen or not go according to plan?

671. What risks might negatively or positively affect achieving the Digital Business Model project objectives?

672. What could prevent you delivering on the strategic program objectives and what is being done to mitigate corresponding issues?

673. Preventative actions - planned actions to reduce the likelihood a risk will occur and/or reduce the seriousness should it occur. What should you do now?

2.33 Probability and Impact Assessment: Digital Business Model

674. Have decisions that should be left open because of inadequate information on technology been identified and responsibility assigned for reducing the uncertainty?

675. What are the levels of understanding of the future users of the outcome/results of this Digital Business Model project?

676. How completely has the customer been identified?

677. Is the customer willing to establish rapid communication links with the developer?

678. How solid is the Digital Business Model projection of competitive reaction?

679. How much is the probability of a risk occurring?

680. Are requirements fully understood by the software engineering team and customers?

681. How is the Digital Business Model project going to be managed?

682. Will new information become available during the Digital Business Model project?

683. What will be the environmental impact of the

Digital Business Model project?

684. Who will be in command to monitor and control the performance of the consortium members (consortium leader/client)?

685. Who will be responsible for a slippage?

686. Who are the international/overseas Digital Business Model project partners (equipment supplier/ supplier/consultant/contractor) for this Digital Business Model project?

687. Risks should be identified during which phase of Digital Business Model project management life cycle?

688. Who should be responsible for the monitoring and tracking of the indicators youhave identified?

689. Do you use diagramming techniques to show cause and effect?

690. Are trained personnel, including supervisors and Digital Business Model project managers, available to handle such a large Digital Business Model project?

691. Are the facilities, expertise, resources, and management know-how available to handle the situation?

2.34 Probability and Impact Matrix: Digital Business Model

692. Why do you need to manage Digital Business Model project Risk?

693. What are the channels available for distribution to the customer?

694. Are testing tools available and suitable?

695. What things might go wrong?

696. What is the level of experience available with your organization?

697. How would you suggest monitoring for risk transition indicators?

698. Lay ground work for future returns?

699. How well is the risk understood?

700. Can you handle the investment risk?

701. What should be done with non-critical risks?

702. Is the Digital Business Model project cutting across the entire organization?

703. Do requirements demand the use of new analysis, design, or testing methods?

704. Which of the risk factors can be avoided altogether?

705. Does the Digital Business Model project team have experience with the technology to be implemented?

706. Mandated delivery date?

707. Which should be probably done NEXT?

708. Have you ascribed a level of confidence to every critical technical objective?

709. What is the best method for analysing the risks for different types of Digital Business Model projects?

710. Are the risk data timely and relevant?

2.35 Risk Data Sheet: Digital Business Model

711. Do effective diagnostic tests exist?

712. What will be the consequences if it happens?

713. What will be the consequences if the risk happens?

714. Potential for recurrence?

715. During work activities could hazards exist?

716. How can hazards be reduced?

717. Who has a vested interest in how you perform as your organization (our stakeholders)?

718. Will revised controls lead to tolerable risk levels?

719. Risk of what?

720. Has a sensitivity analysis been carried out?

721. Type of risk identified?

722. What are you weak at and therefore need to do better?

723. What are you trying to achieve (Objectives)?

724. What do you know?

725. Is the data sufficiently specified in terms of the type of failure being analyzed, and its frequency or probability?

726. What were the Causes that contributed?

727. How reliable is the data source?

728. What can happen?

2.36 Procurement Management Plan: Digital Business Model

729. Have Digital Business Model project team accountabilities & responsibilities been clearly defined?

730. Are the appropriate IT resources adequate to meet planned commitments?

731. Are there checklists created to determine if all quality processes are followed?

732. Are estimating assumptions and constraints captured?

733. Are parking lot items captured?

734. Are Digital Business Model project team members committed fulltime?

735. Are metrics used to evaluate and manage Vendors?

736. Has the Digital Business Model project manager been identified?

737. What is the last item a Digital Business Model project manager must do to finalize Digital Business Model project close-out?

738. Are status reports received per the Digital Business Model project Plan?

739. Is Digital Business Model project work proceeding in accordance with the original Digital Business Model project schedule?

740. Are decisions captured in a decisions log?

741. If standardized procurement documents are needed, where can others be found?

742. Does the schedule include Digital Business Model project management time and change request analysis time?

743. Is a pmo (Digital Business Model project management office) in place which provides oversight to the Digital Business Model project?

2.37 Source Selection Criteria: Digital Business Model

744. How can business terms and conditions be improved to yield more effective price competition?

745. What should be considered when developing evaluation standards?

746. Do you have a plan to document consensus results including disposition of any disagreement by individual evaluators?

747. How and when do you enter into Digital Business Model project Procurement Management?

748. What should preproposal conferences accomplish?

749. Team leads: what is your process for assigning ratings?

750. How should the solicitation aspects regarding past performance be structured?

751. Will the technical evaluation factor unnecessarily force the acquisition into a higher-priced market segment?

752. What should clarifications include?

753. Who is entitled to a debriefing?

754. How important is cost in the source selection decision relative to past performance and technical considerations?

755. With the rapid changes in information technology, will media be readable in five or ten years?

756. How will you evaluate offerors proposals?

757. How can the methods of publicizing the buy be tailored to yield more effective price competition?

758. Are there any specific considerations that precludes offers from being selected as the awardee?

759. Are types/quantities of material, facilities appropriate?

760. Is a letter of commitment from each proposed team member and key subcontractor included?

761. What past performance information should be requested?

762. Does the evaluation of any change include an impact analysis; how will the change affect the scope, time, cost, and quality of the goods or services being provided?

763. Is this a cost contract?

2.38 Stakeholder Management Plan: Digital Business Model

764. Is there a formal set of procedures supporting Issues Management?

765. Are procurement deliverables arriving on time and to specification?

766. Are schedule deliverables actually delivered?

767. Have the procedures for identifying budget variances been followed?

768. What process was used to identify risks to the Digital Business Model projects success?

769. Are risk triggers captured?

770. Are meeting minutes captured and sent out after the meeting?

771. Have external dependencies been captured in the schedule?

772. Are the quality tools and methods identified in the Quality Plan appropriate to the Digital Business Model project?

773. Have all involved stakeholders and work groups committed to the Digital Business Model project?

774. Will all relevant stakeholders be included within

the review process?

775. Are the people assigned to the Digital Business Model project sufficiently qualified?

776. Are stakeholders aware and supportive of the principles and practices of modern software estimation?

777. Are updated Digital Business Model project time & resource estimates reasonable based on the current Digital Business Model project stage?

778. What conditions make using three-point estimating justifiable?

2.39 Change Management Plan: Digital Business Model

779. Is there an adequate supply of people for the new roles?

780. Has the target training audience been identified and nominated?

781. When to start change management?

782. Do there need to be new channels developed?

783. What work practices will be affected?

784. Have the systems been configured and tested?

785. What are the current methods of sharing information and do there need to be new ones developed?

786. What prerequisite knowledge or training is required?

787. What are the major changes to processes?

788. Has the relevant business unit been notified of installation and support requirements?

789. Who might be able to help you the most?

790. Who is responsible for which tasks?

791. What are the training strategies?

792. Change invariability confront many relationships especially the already stated that require a set of behaviours What roles with in your organization are affected and how?

793. How prevalent is Resistance to Change?

794. Do you need new systems?

795. What are the dependencies?

796. Will the culture embrace or reject this change?

797. Do the proposed users have access to the appropriate documentation?

798. Who will fund the training?

3.0 Executing Process Group: Digital Business Model

799. What is involved in the solicitation process?

800. Will new hardware or software be required for servers or client machines?

801. What type of information goes in the quality assurance plan?

802. Is the Digital Business Model project making progress in helping to achieve the set results?

803. What areas does the group agree are the biggest success on the Digital Business Model project?

804. What were things that you did very well and want to do the same again on the next Digital Business Model project?

805. Mitigate. what will you do to minimize the impact should a risk event occur?

806. How do you enter durations, link tasks, and view critical path information?

807. It under budget or over budget?

808. Does the Digital Business Model project team have the right skills?

809. How is Digital Business Model project

performance information created and distributed?

810. What is the shortest possible time it will take to complete this Digital Business Model project?

811. When do you share the scorecard with managers?

812. How do you prevent staff are just doing busywork to pass the time?

813. What areas were overlooked on this Digital Business Model project?

814. Based on your Digital Business Model project communication management plan, what worked well?

815. What are the key components of the Digital Business Model project communications plan?

3.1 Team Member Status Report: Digital Business Model

816. How much risk is involved?

817. Are your organizations Digital Business Model projects more successful over time?

818. Does the product, good, or service already exist within your organization?

819. How will resource planning be done?

820. How can you make it practical?

821. How does this product, good, or service meet the needs of the Digital Business Model project and your organization as a whole?

822. Is there evidence that staff is taking a more professional approach toward management of your organizations Digital Business Model projects?

823. What specific interest groups do you have in place?

824. Does every department have to have a Digital Business Model project Manager on staff?

825. When a teams productivity and success depend on collaboration and the efficient flow of information, what generally fails them?

826. Why is it to be done?

827. Are the products of your organizations Digital Business Model projects meeting customers objectives?

828. How it is to be done?

829. What is to be done?

830. Does your organization have the means (staff, money, contract, etc.) to produce or to acquire the product, good, or service?

831. Will the staff do training or is that done by a third party?

832. The problem with Reward & Recognition Programs is that the truly deserving people all too often get left out. How can you make it practical?

833. Do you have an Enterprise Digital Business Model project Management Office (EPMO)?

834. Are the attitudes of staff regarding Digital Business Model project work improving?

3.2 Change Request: Digital Business Model

835. Will this change conflict with other requirements changes (e.g., lead to conflicting operational scenarios)?

836. Has the change been highlighted and documented in the CSCI?

837. Who is responsible to authorize changes?

838. How do team members communicate with each other?

839. When to submit a change request?

840. Are there requirements attributes that are strongly related to the occurrence of defects and failures?

841. Change request coordination ?

842. When do you create a change request?

843. How well do experienced software developers predict software change?

844. Have all related configuration items been properly updated?

845. Who can suggest changes?

846. Why do you want to have a change control system?

847. Has a formal technical review been conducted to assess technical correctness?

848. What are the requirements for urgent changes?

849. What can be filed?

850. What are the duties of the change control team?

851. How is quality being addressed on the Digital Business Model project?

852. What should be regulated in a change control operating instruction?

853. What is the purpose of change control?

854. Who needs to approve change requests?

3.3 Change Log: Digital Business Model

855. Is the change request open, closed or pending?

856. Who initiated the change request?

857. Is the change request within Digital Business Model project scope?

858. How does this change affect scope?

859. When was the request submitted?

860. Is the change backward compatible without limitations?

861. Is this a mandatory replacement?

862. Is the requested change request a result of changes in other Digital Business Model project(s)?

863. Do the described changes impact on the integrity or security of the system?

864. How does this change affect the timeline of the schedule?

865. Is the submitted change a new change or a modification of a previously approved change?

866. Where do changes come from?

867. Will the Digital Business Model project fail if the change request is not executed?

868. Does the suggested change request seem to represent a necessary enhancement to the product?

869. How does this relate to the standards developed for specific business processes?

870. Should a more thorough impact analysis be conducted?

871. When was the request approved?

872. Does the suggested change request represent a desired enhancement to the products functionality?

3.4 Decision Log: Digital Business Model

873. How does an increasing emphasis on cost containment influence the strategies and tactics used?

874. How consolidated and comprehensive a story can you tell by capturing currently available incident data in a central location and through a log of key decisions during an incident?

875. How does the use a Decision Support System influence the strategies/tactics or costs?

876. How effective is maintaining the log at facilitating organizational learning?

877. Which variables make a critical difference?

878. Meeting purpose; why does this team meet?

879. Who is the decisionmaker?

880. Does anything need to be adjusted?

881. Decision-making process; how will the team make decisions?

882. What alternatives/risks were considered?

883. How does provision of information, both in terms of content and presentation, influence acceptance of

alternative strategies?

884. What is your overall strategy for quality control / quality assurance procedures?

885. What is the average size of your matters in an applicable measurement?

886. What makes you different or better than others companies selling the same thing?

887. At what point in time does loss become unacceptable?

888. Behaviors; what are guidelines that the team has identified that will assist them with getting the most out of team meetings?

889. How do you know when you are achieving it?

890. What was the rationale for the decision?

891. What are the cost implications?

892. It becomes critical to track and periodically revisit both operational effectiveness; Are you noticing all that you need to, and are you interpreting what you see effectively?

3.5 Quality Audit: Digital Business Model

893. Are there appropriate means for intervening if necessary?

894. How does your organization know that its general support services planning and management systems are appropriately effective and constructive?

895. How does your organization know that its staff financial services are appropriately effective and constructive?

896. How does your organization know that its security arrangements are appropriately effective and constructive?

897. How does your organization know that its staff are presenting original work, and properly acknowledging the work of others?

898. Has a written procedure been established to identify devices during all stages of receipt, reconditioning, distribution and installation so that mix-ups are prevented?

899. How does the organization know that its industry and community engagement planning and management systems are appropriately effective and constructive in enabling relationships with key stakeholder groups?

900. Are all employees made aware of device defects which may occur from the improper performance of specific jobs?

901. How does your organization ensure that equipment is appropriately maintained and producing valid results?

902. How does your organization know that the support for its staff is appropriately effective and constructive?

903. How does your organization know that its public relations and marketing systems are appropriately effective and constructive?

904. Is there a written procedure for receiving materials?

905. Have personnel cleanliness and health requirements been established?

906. How does your organization know that its systems for meeting staff extracurricular learning support requirements are appropriately effective and constructive?

907. Are storage areas and reconditioning operations designed to prevent mix-ups and assure orderly handling of both the distressed and reconditioned devices?

908. How does your organization know that its systems for providing high quality consultancy services to external parties are appropriately effective and constructive?

909. How are you auditing your organizations compliance with regulations?

910. Are all employees including salespersons made aware that they must report all complaints received from any source for inclusion in the complaint handling system?

911. Health and safety arrangements; stress management workshops. How does your organization know that it provides a safe and healthy environment?

912. How does your organization know that its staffing profile is optimally aligned with the capability requirements implicit (or explicit) in its Strategic Plan?

3.6 Team Directory: Digital Business Model

913. Process decisions: do invoice amounts match accepted work in place?

914. What needs to be communicated?

915. Process decisions: are there any statutory or regulatory issues relevant to the timely execution of work?

916. What are you going to deliver or accomplish?

917. Contract requirements complied with?

918. When will you produce deliverables?

919. Who will write the meeting minutes and distribute?

920. How will you accomplish and manage the objectives?

921. Process decisions: how well was task order work performed?

922. Process decisions: which organizational elements and which individuals will be assigned management functions?

923. Does a Digital Business Model project team directory list all resources assigned to the Digital

Business Model project?

924. Why is the work necessary?

925. Process decisions: do job conditions warrant additional actions to collect job information and document on-site activity?

926. Have you decided when to celebrate the Digital Business Model projects completion date?

927. Who will be the stakeholders on your next Digital Business Model project?

928. Decisions: is the most suitable form of contract being used?

929. How do unidentified risks impact the outcome of the Digital Business Model project?

930. How and in what format should information be presented?

931. Decisions: what could be done better to improve the quality of the constructed product?

3.7 Team Operating Agreement: Digital Business Model

932. What types of accommodations will be formulated and put in place for sustaining the team?

933. Must your team members rely on the expertise of other members to complete tasks?

934. Do you post any action items, due dates, and responsibilities on the team website?

935. Do you listen for voice tone and word choice to understand the meaning behind words?

936. How does teaming fit in with overall organizational goals and meet organizational needs?

937. How will you resolve conflict efficiently and respectfully?

938. Did you draft the meeting agenda?

939. To whom do you deliver your services?

940. Do you record meetings for the already stated unable to attend?

941. Seconds for members to respond?

942. What is the number of cases currently teamed?

943. Have you set the goals and objectives of the

team?

944. Do you send out the agenda and meeting materials in advance?

945. Do you solicit member feedback about meetings and what would make them better?

946. What resources can be provided for the team in terms of equipment, space, time for training, protected time and space for meetings, and travel allowances?

947. Do team members reside in more than two countries?

948. Are there more than two functional areas represented by your team?

949. Are there differences in access to communication and collaboration technology based on team member location?

950. Do you upload presentation materials in advance and test the technology?

3.8 Team Performance Assessment: Digital Business Model

951. Social categorization and intergroup behaviour: Does minimal intergroup discrimination make social identity more positive?

952. When does the medium matter?

953. To what degree does the teams work approach provide opportunity for members to engage in open interaction?

954. If you have received criticism from reviewers that your work suffered from method variance, what was the circumstance?

955. To what degree do team members frequently explore the teams purpose and its implications?

956. What are teams?

957. Can familiarity breed backup?

958. Individual task proficiency and team process behavior: what is important for team functioning?

959. Can team performance be reliably measured in simulator and live exercises using the same assessment tool?

960. To what degree will the team ensure that all members equitably share the work essential to the

success of the team?

961. Where to from here?

962. To what degree can team members frequently and easily communicate with one another?

963. To what degree do members articulate the goals beyond the team membership?

964. If you have criticized someones work for method variance in your role as reviewer, what was the circumstance?

965. How do you recognize and praise members for contributions?

966. Do friends perform better than acquaintances?

967. To what degree does the team possess adequate membership to achieve its ends?

968. How do you keep key people outside the group informed about its accomplishments?

969. To what degree are the members clear on what they are individually responsible for and what they are jointly responsible for?

970. To what degree will the approach capitalize on and enhance the skills of all team members in a manner that takes into consideration other demands on members of the team?

3.9 Team Member Performance Assessment: Digital Business Model

971. How will they be formed?

972. What variables that affect team members achievement are within your control?

973. Are the goals SMART ?

974. Does adaptive training work?

975. Can your organization rate by exception and assume that most employees are performing at an acceptable level?

976. What is the Business Management Oversight Process?

977. How should adaptive assessments be implemented?

978. How does your team work together?

979. Does statute or regulation require the job responsibility?

980. How is assessment information achieved, stored?

981. What evaluation results did you have?

982. How do you create a self-sustaining capacity for a collaborative culture?

983. What is the target group for instruction (e.g., individual and collective or small team instruction)?

984. To what degree are the goals ambitious?

985. How effective is training that is delivered through technology-based platforms?

986. How is performance assessment used in making future award decisions including options and extend/compete decisions?

987. What evidence supports your decision-making?

988. What is a general description of the processes under performance measurement and assessment?

989. To what extent are systems and applications (e.g., game engine, mobile device platform) utilized?

990. Where can team members go for more detailed information on performance measurement and assessment?

3.10 Issue Log: Digital Business Model

991. Are the Digital Business Model project issues uniquely identified, including to which product they refer?

992. Which stakeholders are thought leaders, influences, or early adopters?

993. How do you manage human resources?

994. Is the issue log kept in a safe place?

995. What is the impact on the Business Case?

996. In your work, how much time is spent on stakeholder identification?

997. What is a change?

998. What would have to change?

999. What help do you and your team need from the stakeholders?

1000. Do you feel a register helps?

1001. How do you manage communications?

1002. Who is the issue assigned to?

1003. Why not more evaluators?

1004. Who do you turn to if you have questions?

1005. What approaches to you feel are the best ones to use?

1006. Which stakeholders can influence others?

1007. What are the typical contents?

1008. What is the stakeholders political influence?

4.0 Monitoring and Controlling Process Group: Digital Business Model

1009. Who are the Digital Business Model project stakeholders?

1010. Just how important is your work to the overall success of the Digital Business Model project?

1011. How many potential communications channels exist on the Digital Business Model project?

1012. How is agile portfolio management done?

1013. What is the expected monetary value of the Digital Business Model project?

1014. Change, where should you look for problems?

1015. Are the necessary foundations in place to ensure the sustainability of the results of the programme?

1016. Feasibility: how much money, time, and effort can you put into this?

1017. Where is the Risk in the Digital Business Model project?

1018. Contingency planning. if a risk event occurs, what will you do?

1019. Have operating capacities been created and/or reinforced in partners?

1020. Were decisions made in a timely manner?

1021. Did the Digital Business Model project team have enough people to execute the Digital Business Model project plan?

1022. Who needs to be involved in the planning?

1023. Is it what was agreed upon?

1024. What business situation is being addressed?

1025. What are the goals of the program?

1026. Were sponsors and decision makers available when needed outside regularly scheduled meetings?

1027. Do the partners have sufficient financial capacity to keep up the benefits produced by the programme?

4.1 Project Performance Report: Digital Business Model

1028. To what degree do the goals specify concrete team work products?

1029. What is the degree to which rules govern information exchange between groups?

1030. To what degree are the tasks requirements reflected in the flow and storage of information?

1031. To what degree are fresh input and perspectives systematically caught and added (for example, through information and analysis, new members, and senior sponsors)?

1032. To what degree can the cognitive capacity of individuals accommodate the flow of information?

1033. To what degree are sub-teams possible or necessary?

1034. To what degree will team members, individually and collectively, commit time to help themselves and others learn and develop skills?

1035. To what degree does the teams approach to its work allow for modification and improvement over time?

1036. To what degree is the team cognizant of small wins to be celebrated along the way?

1037. To what degree are the goals realistic?

1038. What is the degree to which rules govern information exchange between individuals within your organization?

1039. Next Steps?

1040. To what degree do team members understand one anothers roles and skills?

1041. How can Digital Business Model project sustainability be maintained?

1042. How is the data used?

1043. To what degree does the teams work approach provide opportunity for members to engage in fact-based problem solving?

4.2 Variance Analysis: Digital Business Model

1044. Does the scheduling system identify in a timely manner the status of work?

1045. Is the entire contract planned in time-phased control accounts to the extent practicable?

1046. Are significant decision points, constraints, and interfaces identified as key milestones?

1047. Are there changes in the overhead pool and/or organization structures?

1048. Did a new competitor enter the market?

1049. What is the actual cost of work performed?

1050. How have the setting and use of standards changed over time?

1051. How do you evaluate the impact of schedule changes, work around, et?

1052. What are the actual costs to date?

1053. Who are responsible for overhead performance control of related costs?

1054. Do work packages consist of discrete tasks which are adequately described?

1055. Are all cwbs elements specified for external reporting?

1056. Does the contractor use objective results, design reviews and tests to trace schedule performance?

1057. What causes selling price variance?

1058. What costs are avoidable if one or more customers are dropped?

1059. Why are standard cost systems used?

1060. At what point should variances be isolated and brought to the attention of the management?

1061. Are procedures for variance analysis documented and consistently applied at the control account level and selected WBS and organizational levels at least monthly as a routine task?

4.3 Earned Value Status: Digital Business Model

1062. Are you hitting your Digital Business Model projects targets?

1063. Validation is a process of ensuring that the developed system will actually achieve the stakeholders desired outcomes; Are you building the right product? What do you validate?

1064. Verification is a process of ensuring that the developed system satisfies the stakeholders agreements and specifications; Are you building the product right? What do you verify?

1065. Earned value can be used in almost any Digital Business Model project situation and in almost any Digital Business Model project environment. it may be used on large Digital Business Model projects, medium sized Digital Business Model projects, tiny Digital Business Model projects (in cut-down form), complex and simple Digital Business Model projects and in any market sector. some people, of course, know all about earned value, they have used it for years - but perhaps not as effectively as they could have?

1066. What is the unit of forecast value?

1067. How does this compare with other Digital Business Model projects?

1068. If earned value management (EVM) is so good in determining the true status of a Digital Business Model project and Digital Business Model project its completion, why is it that hardly any one uses it in information systems related Digital Business Model projects?

1069. When is it going to finish?

1070. How much is it going to cost by the finish?

1071. Where is evidence-based earned value in your organization reported?

1072. Where are your problem areas?

4.4 Risk Audit: Digital Business Model

1073. How do you govern assets?

1074. Does your organization have or has considered the need for insurance covers: public liability, professional indemnity and directors and officers liability?

1075. Does your auditor understand your business?

1076. Are you aware of the industry standards that apply to your operations?

1077. Is all expenditure authorised through an identified process?

1078. Have you reviewed your constitution within the last twelve months?

1079. What expertise does the Board have on quality, outcomes, and errors?

1080. Can analytical tests provide evidence that is as strong as evidence from traditional substantive tests?

1081. Level of preparation and skill?

1082. Do you record and file all audits?

1083. Do you have a clear plan for the future that describes what you want to do and how you are going to do it?

1084. What limitations do auditors face in effectively applying risk-assessment results to the risk of material misstatement measures?

1085. Do you have a mechanism for managing change?

1086. How can the strategy fail/achieved?

1087. What are the outcomes you are looking for?

1088. Does your organization have an up-to-date constitution?

1089. Does willful intent modify risk-based auditing?

1090. Have risks been considered with an insurance broker or provider and suitable insurance cover been arranged?

4.5 Contractor Status Report: Digital Business Model

1091. Who can list a Digital Business Model project as organization experience, your organization or a previous employee of your organization?

1092. What was the final actual cost?

1093. How long have you been using the services?

1094. What are the minimum and optimal bandwidth requirements for the proposed solution?

1095. If applicable; describe your standard schedule for new software version releases. Are new software version releases included in the standard maintenance plan?

1096. What is the average response time for answering a support call?

1097. Are there contractual transfer concerns?

1098. What was the actual budget or estimated cost for your organizations services?

1099. What process manages the contracts?

1100. Describe how often regular updates are made to the proposed solution. Are corresponding regular updates included in the standard maintenance plan?

1101. What was the budget or estimated cost for your organizations services?

1102. How is risk transferred?

1103. What was the overall budget or estimated cost?

4.6 Formal Acceptance: Digital Business Model

1104. What lessons were learned about your Digital Business Model project management methodology?

1105. Was business value realized?

1106. What is the Acceptance Management Process?

1107. What was done right?

1108. Does it do what client said it would?

1109. Have all comments been addressed?

1110. Did the Digital Business Model project manager and team act in a professional and ethical manner?

1111. Was the Digital Business Model project work done on time, within budget, and according to specification?

1112. How well did the team follow the methodology?

1113. Was the client satisfied with the Digital Business Model project results?

1114. What features, practices, and processes proved to be strengths or weaknesses?

1115. Do you perform formal acceptance or burn-in tests?

1116. Was the Digital Business Model project goal achieved?

1117. Was the sponsor/customer satisfied?

1118. How does your team plan to obtain formal acceptance on your Digital Business Model project?

1119. Do you buy pre-configured systems or build your own configuration?

1120. Do you buy-in installation services?

1121. Who supplies data?

1122. What are the requirements against which to test, Who will execute?

1123. Did the Digital Business Model project achieve its MOV?

5.0 Closing Process Group: Digital Business Model

1124. What areas were overlooked on this Digital Business Model project?

1125. How will you do it?

1126. What were things that you did very well and want to do the same again on the next Digital Business Model project?

1127. Did the Digital Business Model project team have enough people to execute the Digital Business Model project plan?

1128. When will the Digital Business Model project be done?

1129. Does the close educate others to improve performance?

1130. Did the Digital Business Model project management methodology work?

1131. Did the delivered product meet the specified requirements and goals of the Digital Business Model project?

1132. What were the desired outcomes?

1133. Just how important is your work to the overall success of the Digital Business Model project?

1134. What were the actual outcomes?

1135. What areas were overlooked on this Digital Business Model project?

1136. What is the Digital Business Model project name and date of completion?

1137. Based on your Digital Business Model project communication management plan, what worked well?

1138. How will staff learn how to use the deliverables?

1139. How well did the team follow the chosen processes?

5.1 Procurement Audit: Digital Business Model

1140. Was the award criterion only the most economical advantageous tender?

1141. Did the conditions of contract comply with the detail provided in the procurement documents and with the outcome of the procurement procedure followed?

1142. Has it been determined which areas of procurement the audit should cover?

1143. Do at least two people have custodial responsibilities for negotiable checks (one checking on the other)?

1144. Did your organization decide for an appropriate and admissible procurement procedure?

1145. Does the procurement Digital Business Model project comply with European Communities regulations and rules?

1146. How do you address the risk of fraud and corruption?

1147. Do buyers obtain price quotations or bids from two or more suppliers on significant purchases if catalog or advertised prices are not available?

1148. Is the chosen supplier part of your organizations

database?

1149. Is the opportunity properly published?

1150. Do you learn from benchmarking your own practices with international standards?

1151. Are staff members evaluated in accordance with the terms of existing negotiated agreements?

1152. Where your organization engaged an expert, was the contract awarded in compliance with procurement regulations?

1153. Is there a purchasing policy as to the amount of an order on which bidding is required?

1154. Is there a general policy on approval of purchases?

1155. What are the required standards of quality assurance or environmental management?

1156. Are criteria and sub-criteria set suitable to identify the tender that offers best value for money?

1157. Were any additional works or deliveries admissible without the need for a new procurement procedure?

1158. Does the department have a procurement strategy and is it implemented?

1159. Is it calculated whether aggregated procurement can be more cost-efficient?

5.2 Contract Close-Out: Digital Business Model

1160. Parties: who is involved?

1161. How/when used ?

1162. How is the contracting office notified of the automatic contract close-out?

1163. Change in knowledge?

1164. Change in circumstances?

1165. How does it work?

1166. Change in attitude or behavior?

1167. Are the signers the authorized officials?

1168. Have all contracts been completed?

1169. Why Outsource?

1170. Was the contract type appropriate?

1171. Has each contract been audited to verify acceptance and delivery?

1172. Have all contracts been closed?

1173. Parties: Authorized?

1174. Have all contract records been included in the Digital Business Model project archives?

1175. Was the contract complete without requiring numerous changes and revisions?

1176. Was the contract sufficiently clear so as not to result in numerous disputes and misunderstandings?

1177. Have all acceptance criteria been met prior to final payment to contractors?

1178. What happens to the recipient of services?

1179. What is capture management?

5.3 Project or Phase Close-Out: Digital Business Model

1180. Was the schedule met?

1181. What can you do better next time, and what specific actions can you take to improve?

1182. What is a Risk?

1183. What is the information level of detail required for each stakeholder?

1184. What security considerations needed to be addressed during the procurement life cycle?

1185. What could have been improved?

1186. If you were the Digital Business Model project sponsor, how would you determine which Digital Business Model project team(s) and/or individuals deserve recognition?

1187. What benefits or impacts does the stakeholder group expect to obtain as a result of the Digital Business Model project?

1188. What are the marketing communication needs for each stakeholder?

1189. Which changes might a stakeholder be required to make as a result of the Digital Business Model project?

1190. What are they?

1191. In addition to assessing whether the Digital Business Model project was successful, it is equally critical to analyze why it was or was not fully successful. Are you including this?

1192. Did the Digital Business Model project management methodology work?

1193. Is there a clear cause and effect between the activity and the lesson learned?

1194. Is the lesson significant, valid, and applicable?

1195. Can the lesson learned be replicated?

1196. Who controlled key decisions that were made?

1197. Who is responsible for award close-out?

5.4 Lessons Learned: Digital Business Model

1198. What policy constraints are relevant?

1199. What are the performance measures?

1200. How much flexibility is there in the funding (e.g., what authorities does the program manager have to change to the specifics of the funding within the overall funding ceiling)?

1201. What on the Digital Business Model project worked well and was effective in the delivery of the product?

1202. Did the delivered product meet the specified requirements and goals of the Digital Business Model project?

1203. How adaptable is the deliverable?

1204. How will you allocate your funding resources?

1205. How effective was the architecture/system design process?

1206. What regulatory regime controlled how your organization head and program manager directed your organization and Digital Business Model project?

1207. How do individuals resolve conflict?

1208. How effectively and timely was your organizational change impact identified and planned for?

1209. What is the frequency of group communications?

1210. Were the Digital Business Model project goals attained?

1211. What is the distribution of authority?

1212. How useful was the format and content of the Digital Business Model project Status Report to you?

1213. What is below the surface?

1214. How effective were your functional specs?

1215. Recommendation: what do you recommend should be done to ensure that others throughout your organization can benefit from what you have learned?

1216. How well does the product or service the Digital Business Model project produced meet the defined Digital Business Model project requirements?

1217. What is the value of the deliverable?

Index

CPSIA information can be obtained
at www.ICGtesting.com
Printed in the USA
BVHW041214170719
553686BV00012B/291/P